THE ZOMBIES ARE COMING

THE REALITIES OF THE ZOMBIE APOCALYPSE IN AMERICAN CULTURE
REVISED AND EXPANDED EDITION

THE ZOMBIES ARE COMING

**THE REALITIES OF THE ZOMBIE
APOCALYPSE IN AMERICAN CULTURE**
REVISED AND EXPANDED EDITION

KELLY J. BAKER

Blue Crow Books

Copyright © 2020 by Kelly J. Baker
All rights reserved.
No part of this book may be reproduced in any form or by any electronic or mechanical means, including information storage and retrieval systems, without written permission from the author, except for the use of brief quotations in a book review.

Publisher's Cataloging-in-Publication Data
Baker, Kelly J. 1980-.
The Zombies Are Coming: The Realities of the Zombie Apocalypse in American Culture, Revised and Expanded Edition / Kelly J. Baker
p.____ cm.____
ISBN 978-1-947834-49-1 (Pbk.) | 978-1-947834-50-7 (Ebook)
1. Apocalypse in mass media. 2. Zombies in popular culture. 3. Eschatology. I. Title.
814.6 | PCN 2020937107

Published by Blue Crow Books
an imprint of Blue Crow Publishing, LLC
Chapel Hill, NC
www.bluecrowpublishing.com
Cover photo: tetrebbien via Unsplash.com
Cover Design by Lauren Faulkenberry

ALSO BY KELLY J. BAKER

Gospel According to the Klan: The KKK's Appeal to Protestant America, 1915-1930

Grace Period: A Memoir in Pieces

Sexism Ed: Essays on Gender and Labor in Academia

Succeeding Outside the Academy: Career Paths Beyond the Humanities, Social Sciences, and STEM

The Zombies Are Coming: The Realities of the Zombie Apocalypse in American Culture (Revised and Expanded Edition)

Final Girl: And Other Essays on Grief, Trauma, and Mental Illness

PRAISE FOR KELLY J. BAKER

PRAISE FOR GRACE PERIOD

Baker deftly balances personal struggles and broad institutional inequities as she confronts the trauma of leaving the academy. Her journey will help many traverse their own paths forward.

— KAREN KELSKY, AUTHOR OF *THE PROFESSOR IS IN: THE ESSENTIAL GUIDE TO TURNING YOUR PH.D. INTO A JOB*

A book about dreams: what they give us, what they take from us, how they break us, and how they re-make us.

— *THE TALLAHASSEE DEMOCRAT*

A series of vivid and beautiful essays.

— *BOOK RIOT*

PRAISE FOR SEXISM ED

An absolute must-read. *Sexism Ed* tells savage truths that every administrator and tenured prof should be forced to read and acknowledge.

— MARC BOUSQUET, AUTHOR OF *HOW THE UNIVERSITY WORKS: HIGHER EDUCATION AND THE LOW-WAGE NATION*

A meticulously sourced and thorough look into the myriad ways that misogyny is built into the very bones of the academy, not some sad by-product of it.

— JESSICA W. LUTHER, AUTHOR OF *UNSPORTSMANLIKE CONDUCT: COLLEGE FOOTBALL AND THE POLITICS OF RAPE*

Harrowing, though never humorless or hopeless, this collection is required reading.

— KECIA ALI, AUTHOR OF *SEXUAL ETHICS AND ISLAM: FEMINIST REFLECTIONS ON QUR'AN, HADITH, AND JURISPRUDENCE*

In a stirring suite of essays, Kelly Baker reveals that, contrary to its "ivory tower" characterization, the university is no retreat from the world's injustices.

— MIYA TOKUMITSU, AUTHOR OF *DO WHAT YOU LOVE: AND OTHER LIES ABOUT SUCCESS & HAPPINESS*

A window into sexual politics, the academy, and the structures of inequity that are this American moment.

— LAURA LEVITT, AUTHOR OF *JEWS AND FEMINISM: THE AMBIVALENT SEARCH FOR HOME AND AMERICAN JEWISH LOSS AFTER THE HOLOCAUST*

PRAISE FOR THE ZOMBIES ARE COMING

Baker reminds us that apocalyptic fantasies have always been part of the popular American imagination.

— KATHRYN REKLIS, AUTHOR OF *THEOLOGY AND THE KINESTHETIC IMAGINATION: JONATHAN EDWARDS AND THE MAKING OF MODERNITY*

Reveals the deep ambivalence about modern culture the zombie apocalypse obsession suggests.

— W. SCOTT POOLE, AWARD-WINNING AUTHOR OF *MONSTERS IN AMERICA: OUR HISTORICAL OBSESSION WITH THE HIDEOUS AND THE HAUNTING*

A perfect guide through the unrelenting, decaying hordes of our contemporary zombie apocalypse.

— SEAN MCCLOUD, AUTHOR OF *AMERICAN POSSESSIONS: FIGHTING DEMONS IN THE CONTEMPORARY UNITED STATES*

As only she can, Baker lures readers down pop culture's dark alleyways, riddling out our inability to get over the end of the world or what comes after. This book is a jagged mirror held up to America's violent fantasies, deepest fears, and addiction to apocalypses—forcing us to admit that the real monsters just might be the homicidal misogyny, bloodthirsty white supremacy, and rabid consumerism we made along the way.

— MEGAN GOODWIN, AUTHOR OF
ABUSING RELIGION: LITERARY PERSECUTION, SEX SCANDALS, AND AMERICAN MINORITY RELIGIONS

To Kara and Ethan, who make me think about what other worlds are possible instead of dwelling on the ends of ours

(And to Chris, the person I would fight all the zombies for)

[A] culture's main task is to survive its own imaginative demise.
  —Edward Ingebretsen, *At Stake*[1]

People have always been good at imagining the end of the world, which is much easier to picture than the strange sidelong paths of change in a world without end.
  —Rebecca Solnit, *Hope in the Dark*[2]

Dear Lord, please let there be a zombie apocalypse so I can start shooting all these motherfuckers in the face.
  —someecards user card

CONTENTS

Foreword: "Extreme Zombie Activity"	xvii
1. Introduction: "Mommy, zombies aren't real." *Zombies and the End of the World*	1
2. "Apocalypse Obsession." *Apocalypticism's Past and Present*	17
3. "It's going to be a federal incident." *The CDC and the DHS Prepare for Zombies*	48
4. "No Joke, the Zombie Apocalypse Is Coming!" *The Summer of the Walking Dead*	64
5. "Are you able to shoot your kid in the face?" *Doomsday Preppers and the Zombie Apocalypse*	76
6. "We hate ALL zombies." *The Intimate Relationship Between Zombies and Guns*	98
Afterword: "You've Got Some Red on You."	119
Interview in TheoFantastique	129
Interview in Religion Bulletin	137
Notes	147
Acknowledgments	155
About the Author	159

FOREWORD: "EXTREME ZOMBIE ACTIVITY"
Zombies, Horror, and Us

[W]e make up horrors to help us cope with real ones.
—Stephen King[1]

In May of 2018, it happened again: An actual warning about zombies popped up in my inbox, and I couldn't help but click. (Since at least 2010, I have had a Google Alert set to keep track of any mention of the shambling undead.) It was almost a familiar story, but instead of a hacked road sign, it was a hacked emergency bulletin sent out to residents of Lake Worth, Florida. It's a city just over 484 miles away from the place I live now in Florida.

The Huffington Post reported that the alert, sent after one o'clock on a Sunday morning, warned of a "power outage and zombie alert" for the city. The cause of all this was due to "extreme zombie activity." The alert was an automatic one, which goes out after any outage to residents. This, however, was not an approved message. It was a joke that some Lake Worth residents took seriously as an actual warning. Susan Leighton of *Fansided* noted that city officials were "flooded with messages" from "terrified residents." The threat of "extreme zombie activity" likely conjured images straight from a George Romero movie with the dead rising up and feasting on humans.

The city's public information officer later stated on *Lake Worth Live*, "I want to reiterate that Lake Worth does not have any zombie activity currently," and he apologized for the rogue message.[2]

Watch out for zombies, *as if.*

Of course, this was not the first or second or third instance of hackers managing to fake a warning about the imminent threat of zombies, and I doubt it will be the last. Electronic road signs are an easy target, though the hacked signs haven't often happened in Florida, the state of my birth and where I managed to end up again. And yet, all of a sudden there was the threat of extreme zombie activity in my state of all places. (And I know what you all are thinking: Of course, it would be Florida because of its wild but also accurate reputation. Florida is a state known for its bizarreness, and the ubiquitous Florida man that makes the national news).

I wasn't surprised by Florida since I am resigned to

the strange things that happen here. I wasn't surprised by the alert because similar enough things had happened before. Instead, I was remarkably intrigued by how the public information officer emphasized that there was no zombie activity *currently*, as if the monsters might appear at any other time in the near future. As if the dead rising could happen at any moment. As if the zombie apocalypse—the end of the world by monsters—could be just around the corner but not right now. As if the zombie apocalypse was a possibility rather than a fantasy, which we watch play out on screens—big and small. As if extreme zombie activity could happen, but not right now. As if Romero's monsters could be an actual threat, not just a prank.

It's fitting, fortuitous even, I thought, *that this would happen while I was working on this very book about those Americans who believe, hope for, and prepare for the zombie apocalypse.*

Seven years ago, when I began writing *The Zombies Are Coming*, the earlier version of this book, it was abundantly clear that the zombie apocalypse was a common, mundane even, fixture in American popular culture. There were novels, books, video games, and TV shows. My then-students wanted to talk to me about the most recent zombie film they had watched and wanted to know what I thought about the perennial debate over fast versus slow zombies. (Who wants fast zombies when the slow ones conjure creeping demise in ways that you can't shake?) They were well-versed in fictional zombies and their dystopian consequences for worlds that closely resembled our own. They watched *The Walking Dead* and George Romero's classic zombie films. They played *Resident Evil* and were looking forward to *The Last of Us* (released in June of 2013). And, so many of them loved zombies, unabashedly and deeply, and they wanted me to love them too. Zombies, they told me again and again, were so much *fun*.

But perhaps you don't love zombies or find them fun. Perhaps you aren't even familiar with the zombie apocalypse genre. That's okay. Really. If you aren't familiar, here's the short version: Something bad happens—often we don't know what exactly—and the dead reanimate with a grisly hunger for human brains or flesh. These monsters quickly bring about the end of the world as we've come to know it. Suddenly, there's no electricity. Our cellphones, which we rely on to navigate the world, run out of bars and batteries. Infrastructure manages to instantly crumble. All the laws and social norms that govern our behavior disappear as survivors try to escape the ravenous horde.

Chaos rules; order is long gone.

The zombie apocalypse is another end of the world scenario, a heady mash-up of horror and survival stories. The themes and motifs feel like they come straight out of westerns that I watched as a kid—justified violence, dangers lurking in nature and in the people you encounter, survival of the fittest, and rugged masculinity—paired with societal breakdown and previously-human-but-now-monsters.

The zombie apocalypse is not a genre for the faint of heart; it's gruesome, violent, and bleak. The plots follow a familiar and predictable rhythm: The dead won't remain dead, society falls, and the few humans that remain make torturous attempts to survive in a ruined world that might not be able to be saved. These stories are blood-soaked and gore-obsessed. Monsters harm, maim, and brutally kill humans, and humans harm, maim, and brutally kill monsters and other humans with occasional attempts at moral justification but mostly the suggestion of the necessity of violence to solve all problems.

Humans also destroy monsters with guns, knives, swords, crossbows, bats, more guns, and other more creative weapons, a la flinging records at the monsters from *Shaun of the Dead* (2004) or dropping a piano on one from *Zombieland* (2009). The zombie apocalypse presents a dystopian tale about the perils of doomsday as well as reflections on what happens to those who remain. What happens if everything goes sideways? What happens to us in the aftermath of a disaster and when society is something we can barely remember? Audiences get a glimpse of what it might take to survive in an unfamiliar, antagonistic landscape.

Novels, films, video games, and television shows portray the world after zombies. This end often looks the same but with a new cast of characters that struggle with this new world. So, what does the world look like at the end? Awful and heart-rending. Who manages to survive? Mostly white people. And why would we even want to survive in this kind of world? I don't know.

My inability to know is part of what motivates this book. I wanted to know who would find the zombie apocalypse appealing enough to hope that it actually happens. I wanted to see their reasons and justifications. I wanted to see if I could understand their motivations.

The other part of what drew me to write about this fascination and yearning for the zombie apocalypse was that horror, especially the genre's cautionary nature and acceptance of how things can go so terribly wrong, was already something that I was mildly obsessed with.

During much of my early life, I was an avid fan of horror, particularly ghost stories. By middle school, I was reading books by R.L. Stine, Christopher Pike, L.J. Smith, Dean Koontz, and Stephen King because I had already read through the novels available at the school library, the public library, or even the book fair. I read these books, even if they made it impossible for me to sleep at night. By high school, I watched any film with monsters, serial killers, or vengeful ghosts. Horror made and continues to make sense to me. It has a pattern that is easy to follow and a stark moralism that makes the world appear simpler than the rather complex world we inhabit.

Some people were victims; others were survivors. And the person who made it through the worst night ever or even the end of the world was most often the person who followed the genre's strict rules and inhabited the right kind of body. (It wasn't hard to realize that people of color didn't last long in horror novels and films, if they were included at all, and neither did sexually active white women. Horror's moralism had a distinctive conservative flair.)

As a young white woman who meticulously followed almost all of the rules, I knew who my people were in horror. I knew who I would be, a girl who lived through the end, even as she might not have wanted to. I also came to expect the gruesome punishment that awaited those who simply didn't follow the crystal-clear rules. Horror made sense because actions had direct, immediate consequences. Terrible people met terrible but expected fates, unlike in everyday life. And yet, it wasn't only the terrible who suffered in horror; ordinary, decent folks met gory ends too.

Horror conveyed how vulnerable we each are; how breakable our bodies can be and are; and even legitimized my anxiety and fear about the world around me. There were things to be afraid of, ordinary and extraordinary, so why not be afraid?

Horror shows us that the world is a more perilous place than most of us think. Things can go awry in a single moment: a missed turn, a stranger at the door, a summer camp trip, a hitchhiker who needs a ride, a new house with a tragic history, a game that turns into something more deadly, or even space radiation that makes corpses rise from their graves. Things go wrong in horror movies, and people die over and over again. In *The Zombie Survival Guide: Complete Protection from the Undead* (2003), Max Brooks reminds us, "Simply put, there are thousands of ways to kill a human—and only one to kill a zombie."[3] Humans are fragile; we can break. Zombies are our (potentially) ruined bodies on clear display.

In horror, the world was obviously dangerous with ominous music, dark and gloomy atmosphere, and doors that should never be opened. These stories were so simple to understand, cause and effect played out on the screen or the page. Horror offered no shades of gray, no complexity or nuance. There was a temporary comfort in knowing that, at least in the fictional universes of horror, rules were enforced and that each movie and book always had to end. The monsters were staked temporarily (because the monster often comes back). We could move on and maybe even sleep soundly again.

It's really no surprise that I started writing about zombie apocalypses and horror in American culture. I was already primed for it.

So, in 2013, when I noticed news story after news story about people acting in bizarre and markedly violent ways that led journalists to compare perpetrators to zombies and ponder (mostly tongue-in-cheek) that the end might actually be nigh, I wondered what in the world was *happening*. When I learned that the Center of Disease Control had an emergency preparedness plan about the zombie apocalypse to cajole people into preparation and planning for actual disasters, I wondered about the usefulness of zombies to do cultural work. When I watched the Discovery Channel's "documentary" about four folks avidly preparing for a doomsday brought about by zombies, I scratched my head and tried to figure out why folks were preparing for movie monsters to attack them. When I came across Zombie Industries' exploding zombie targets, I wasn't sure what to make of the doomsday prep for zombies and the attachments to American gun culture.

Didn't they know that *zombies weren't real*?

Perhaps, it had something to do with the popularity of *The Walking Dead* in its third season in 2013, or the release of *World War Z*, with a rugged, scarf-wearing

Brad Pitt trying to save the world from fast zombies. But that wasn't enough to explain how zombies shifted from fictional threats on small and big screens to an actual one or how this threat could even happen. The popularity and ubiquity of these monsters also didn't explain why some Americans wanted zombies to become *real*.

So, I wanted to consider what happens when a fictional horror—a monster—shifts out of fantasy into reality and what the consequences of that shift might be. I wanted to move from the fairly common focus on movies, books, and TV shows to consider the people who hoped—yearned even—for the zombie apocalypse. Why did the zombie apocalypse appeal to some Americans? And who were these people who wanted something akin to doomsday to happen soon? Why the zombie apocalypse? Why right now?

It wasn't only folks hoping for zombies and the end that piqued my interest. I also wanted to consider all of those people who interpreted contemporary events through the lens of the zombie apocalypse. Why were they relying on plots and narrative tropes from monster movies to explain the news? What did this say about how they interpreted our world? Why did we need horror movies to explain the news to us?

There was a moment from around 2011 to 2013, in which some Americans wanted to avidly *believe* that a zombie apocalypse could be real. These attempts to push fantasy into reality were both fascinating and disconcerting. After all, zombies menaced, harmed, and killed humans in fictional universes. Their pop culture dominance was hard to ignore. And yet, a world, in which zombies and humans existed side-by-side, didn't work out well for humans. Since they proved so dangerous to humans in all the zombie media we consumed, wouldn't they be dangerous to us, if they ever became real? To me, it seemed that they would be without question.

I knew that I sure didn't want to wake up one day to an alert about "extreme zombie activity," which wasn't a joke but an *actual* alert about corpses rising from their graves. My survival would be far from guaranteed. I already suspected that I would be a goner if monsters suddenly appeared on my doorstep. I'm a writer, for goodness sakes, not a survivalist. I have no skills to save me in any apocalyptic scenario. I hate cardio, so even if I tried to run, I wouldn't get far. So, let's be honest: I would be one of the first to be eaten, mostly because my children are morally opposed to being quiet and still.

My reaction was different from those people who did want zombie activity to be extreme. They were ready for the end of the world. And they hoped that maybe, just maybe, zombies could become real. And then, they could kill the monsters with no abandon.

After all, zombies could become real, right? Folks

pointed to examples in nature of supposed zombification. There was a fungus that transformed ants into something other than what they were, something we might describe as zombies. It was a parasite that took over the ants' brains and changed their behaviors.[4] Zombie ants appeared in headline after headline. If it wasn't the ants, there were other supposed incidents of zombies. Newspapers and magazines, online and off, reported on horrific acts of violence, including cannibalism, which seemed beyond the scope of the human. So, the media labeled the perpetrators "zombies" and told stories that appeared as plots to a horror movie rather than an act of violence that could happen in your neighborhood or to some unlucky soul in the wrong place at the wrong time.

And there was also lingering impact of the end of the Mayan calendar in 2012 and so-called prophecies about how the world would end, which zombies could, somehow, be attached to. Doomsday and doomsday predictions were popular and profitable.

But, there seemed to be something about this particular type of end-times scenario, so I wrote about it, even as I wondered whether this fervor could be sustained. I wondered whether it might be a fleeting interest that wouldn't endure. I was writing about a moment of zombie apocalypses that seemed unsustainable. I was writing about a moment that I thought would pass.

I half-heartedly assumed that folks might eventually tire of these shambling—and occasionally fast—monsters bringing about the end of the world. Zombies and their apocalypses had to eventually not entertain us anymore. Some other doomsday would catch our interest, like killer robots, deadly mermaids, sexy vampires, or angsty werewolves. (I vote for mermaids with sharp teeth and claws.) At least, I thought that doomsday preppers would have moved along to different and more likely disaster scenarios, which might have focused on other more pressing threats like climate change, cataclysmic weather patterns, or the finiteness of natural resources.

Fads shift and change. We know this. The popularity of different types of apocalyptic thinking also come and go. Americans are good at predicting one type of doomsday and moving onto another. Zombies might have gone by the wayside too. I kept waiting for them to, but they never did.

Here I am still writing about this type of doomsday because it continues to endure. *The Walking Dead* is in its tenth season and spawned a spin-off show, *Fear the Walking Dead*. Zombie video games come out one after another. The media still reports on humans engaged in violent acts, who they describe as "zombies." And folks still prep for, what they imagine, is our inevitable demise by never-satiated monsters and claim that prepping for this disaster makes them able to handle the Covid-19 pandemic. This wasn't what I would have thought would happen, but reality hardly ever matches my expectations for long or at all.

I can't help but wonder what the continued attachment to the zombie apocalypse means for all of us, in particular, and American culture as a whole. Reworking this book allows me to consider, again, why and how the zombie apocalypse becomes a reality and why some want it to be such. (I am still not on team doomsday.)

When I began writing this book, and even now, I'm still intrigued by the people who blurred the boundaries between those horrors on the screen, or page, and what most of us consider real life. How did the fantasy inform reality? How did they inform one another? What might relying on fantasy, especially brutal fantasy, to interpret our world do for us? Or maybe, the better question is what would it do *to us*?

Fantasy elided into reality; reality elided into fantasy. This continues to happen, unabated.

Monsters from popular culture were not content to destroy fictional worlds over and over again, and they also managed to become potential threats to the world that we all share. (Admittedly, they needed some help to do this.) How could that kind of elision happen? Why did it happen? What was it about zombies that allowed them to slip so easily from fantasy into reality? Moreover, why were some Americans, then and now, hopeful and almost joyous about the prospect of a zombie apocalypse? What did a zombie apocalypse allow them to do that they couldn't right now? What might it offer to them that our world didn't? The zombie apocalypse was doing cultural work for them, and I wanted to know exactly what this work was.

These questions kept returning to me, like the relentless monster, but the one question that I couldn't quite get over was: Why would the zombie apocalypse be something to desire? I struggled to understand. Zombies bring about destruction and ruins; joy seemed like not quite the correct response. I wasn't looking forward to shambling monsters showing up at my house, so I wanted to know more about the people who were. I wanted to understand how and why doomsday held appeal. If I could find an answer to that question of desire and wishing for the end, I figured that I might learn something about American culture, the relationship to the end times, and the role of violence.

Pop culture trains us on how to approach our world and what the dangers that we face might be, and I needed to know what the zombie apocalypse could possibly train us for or whether we really want that kind of training. Some of the answers seemed obvious: a survival-at-all-costs mentality, the glorification of violence, and an overreliance on guns.

And yet, this doomsday scenario also emphasized disaster preparedness and our vulnerabilities to an assortment of calamities, which are things to consider and pay attention to. They seem to offer a different side to the brutality present in zombified ends. They almost seem like a social good.

The more I dug into attempts to realize the zombie apocalypse or to imagine what it would bring, the more I realized the complexities of its appeal. This book began as my attempt to think carefully about why and how apocalypses appeal and why the zombie apocalypse, in particular, appeals to so many.

As a religious studies scholar and analyst of American culture, I also wanted to think about what we could learn about the American present by taking seriously those folks who are apt to be dismissed as too kooky or fringe to study. And make no mistake, the folks who promote doomsday and prophesize its reality are consistently pushed to the margins or explained away as somehow not normal or representative. Both journalists and scholars marginalize these people, but kookiness, in and of itself, is a value judgment and not analysis.

Ideas that might, at first, seem fringe have a tendency to make their way into the mainstream, and sometimes, they were mainstream all along. The so-called fringe and the mainstream are not so clearly demarcated as people often assume. Apocalyptic ideas and themes permeate American culture; they are not limited to the margins. They are popular. They have a history. They prove appealing. They can't be confined to the margins when zombie apocalypses continue to remain popular, and doomsday, more generally, makes Hollywood blockbusters. Making apocalypticism seem strange ignores how it informs our politics and our practices. Doomsday motivates people, so we should know about these motivations and their consequences rather than minimize or dismiss them. Apocalypticism provides a lens to interpret our world with stark, moral clarity and profound sense of who counts as *us* and who becomes *them*. It impacts one's approach to the world, other people, and politics. It can't be ignored or minimized.

Moreover, it's important to pay attention to the way people create, practice, and embody their beliefs, even the ones that seem far-fetched. While some might dismiss belief in the zombie apocalypse as a fantasy with no bearing on reality, human action makes belief *real*. The efforts of those who believe in this flavor of catastrophe help make the zombie apocalypse a reality. It becomes real in government agencies' training events, in emergency preparedness campaigns, in zombie hunting gear and survival kits, and in news stories that rely on narratives of monsters to report on horrific crimes.

People's actions shift zombified ends out of fantasy into reality; their efforts make doomsday appear more and more concrete and tangible.

They make doomsday a possible reality in every story, training, and purchase.

For me, this yearning and preparation for the zombie apocalypse offered a revelation about American culture and its discontents in this moment and the recent past.

If folks hope an apocalypse is upon us and that it can actually *happen*, what must they think of our current world and our future? Perhaps, they see our future as one of inevitable collapse, chaos, and violence rather than a brighter and less blood-soaked one. The end, Rebecca Solnit reminds us, is often easier to imagine than a future. Doom is easier to predict rather than progress.[5] A world destroyed is easier than refashioning our society in a way that it is more just to all people rather than maintaining the status quo that benefits the few over the many. Perhaps, they are just having fun by imagining an end by zombies, a safer threat to ponder due to their unreality. It is not fun to consider the dire consequences of natural disasters or the looming threat of climate change. Perhaps, the answer resides in a harrowing combination of both.

In this book, I consider and reconsider the implications of wishing for zombies to end us. At its heart, this is a book about what it means to prepare for, or avoid, threats to human existence and to choose to prepare for fictional monsters rather than more likely disasters. When we choose zombies, we conveniently avoid *what might actually end us*.

Preparing for fictional monsters is not quite as terrifying as preparing for hurricanes, tornados, earthquakes, fires, floods or a pandemic. Imagining that the end comes from infected mouths and grasping hands means that maybe you don't have to realize that maybe somewhere like Florida, surrounded by rising waters, might have an expiration date. That the place you live in might not exist in the future. That the future is more tenuous than guaranteed. That part of your world might have a time limit. That you also have a time limit.

And yet, horror, fiction, shows us how the shit can hit the fan. In his essay on the importance of horror movies for *Vulture*, David Edelstein writes:

> Seas rise, species die, the Earth is poised to punish humanity for its arrogance....We know that soon enough there will be blood—and gore—and all the other things you can find right now in an average horror movie.[6]

Horror, he explains, shows "more acute versions of our worst-case scenarios," and zombie apocalypses and other horror shows serve as "brilliant metaphors for what haunts us."

So, zombies might be a way to dodge the real and pressing threats that could easily overwhelm us. Zombies could offer a simpler story about our world and its discontent that we prefer rather than the ambiguity and ambivalence that we have to negotiate day in and out. The zombie apocalypse might seem easier to face than what actually awaits us, and perhaps, Edelstein is right. Perhaps, zombies show us a worst-case scenario that lurks around the corner waiting to pounce. Perhaps, zombies are a stand-in for some threat, any threat really. Perhaps, they are a horror story that we need to stop and pay attention to.

Because remember, reader, horror stories are cautionary tales, and this book is about the cautions that zombies bring, in their shambles, moans, and unrelenting hunger. The zombie apocalypse is never a neutral fantasy; it has teeth that rend, maim, and kill. This book, then, is a plea for us to take zombies and their doomsdays seriously. I want us to consider the consequences of some Americans wanting the end of the world to be real. And what that might mean for the rest of us.

Life doesn't easily mesh with the horror story. There's too much complexity and nuance. But some want it to, and they try to make our world fit within horror's confines. They want the monsters to escape. They want the end to happen. They want the blood, gore, and ruins, no matter the consequences. But, the consequences are more dire than they, and maybe you, think. This book is about the consequences for all of us when folks imagine the zombie apocalypse to be real. It's a book about the stakes for our shared world and why we should all care. It's my declaration that what we consider might be only fun is always something more—and might be something dangerous.

The zombies are coming, so pay attention.

Kelly J. Baker
May 2020

1

INTRODUCTION: "MOMMY, ZOMBIES AREN'T REAL."
Zombies and the End of the World

We're being eaten alive by the damned things, and we love it.
—Geoff Pevere[1]

I first believed in the zombie apocalypse in the stairwell of a multi-level parking garage in Knoxville, TN. I had parked in this very garage time and again to visit local shops and restaurants and play at the splash pad with my daughter. I parked there before, but on this particular day—years ago—something strange happened. Despite the sunlight that filled so much of the garage, the stairs between levels were beyond its reach. They were dark, foreboding, and littered with debris. As I started my descent, a vision of shuffling zombies appeared unbidden. Not pasty-faced Romero zombies, but those legitimately terrifying ones from *The Walking Dead*. I began to imagine a small horde of the monsters swarming at the bottom of the stairs and blocking off my potential exit. One vision of zombies proved to not be enough.

As soon as I began thinking about them, I imagined additional scenarios. What if they stumbled down the stairs above me, catching me unaware? What if they had caught me after I exited and locked my car? What if I came face to face with a zombie? What would I do? What would I be able to do? What if I was eaten alive?

My heart beat faster, my palms were sweaty, and my feet moved more quickly from step to step. *This garage*, I realized reluctantly, *would be the perfect place for an undead attack.* Resurrected corpses would end me in a dirty stairwell, and there would be no meaningful death for me. (Is there even such a thing as a meaningful death?) Instead, I would be torn apart by the hands and teeth of ravenous zombies. They would happily munch on my flesh, or brains, without any concern as to how I might feel about the disastrous turn of events. In my last moments, I would be dinner to monsters. Hopefully, I would die quickly.

"Awesome," I muttered, "I really wish I had a baseball bat."

After escaping the stairs shaken but unscathed, the sunny day chased away my fear of zombies, and I turned to my errands. Yet later, I was startled by my own imaginings. Why did zombies, of all things, appear as the looming threat rather than anything that could actually happen—a robbery, a fall (I am remarkably clumsy), or some sort of physical attack?

Frankly, I chided myself, *I should have known better.*

Then, I was the mother of one kid, a preschooler, so I was well-versed in discussions about how monsters were just *make-believe*. I assured her over and over again that zombies, vampires, werewolves, mummies, and ghosts were not real; they were just fantasy. *They don't exist*, I would explain to her almost patiently, *and things that don't exist can't hurt us*. (Or could they?)

As we watched *Hotel Transylvania* (2012) together, we laughed at the hapless monsters, who were mostly silly and only occasionally threatening. And we talked about how these monsters were just cartoons. They were fiction. Zombies didn't exist, and they definitely weren't employed as bellhops at a hotel run by the infamous vampire, Dracula.

Maybe because I reassured her so often, my daughter would also reassure me: "Mommy, zombies, ghosts, and dragons aren't real." I nodded my head in agreement. She and I could both identify fantasy, especially in its scarier forms. Now, I have similar discussions with her brother, almost five years younger than her. He also wants to know if monsters are real. He wants to know if *any* monsters could be real. He wants to know if there are any loopholes to the "monsters don't really exist" rule. Additionally, he likes to remind me that—in spite of the fact that I write about zombies—they are not *really real*. His tone suggests that perhaps, I am not as convincing as I think I am.

And yet, the fear I experienced in the garage, all those years ago, *was* real. When I was confronted with a dark, slightly creepy space, zombies popped up to my overactive imagination as a plausible threat. For a moment, it almost seemed that they could be as real as they were terrifying and that my life could be at stake. For the first time, their reality appeared almost possible to me.

I couldn't help but wonder why. What the hell was happening to me?

My fear was palpable, and it spurred me to crave action, almost violent action. (Let's be honest: I don't even own a baseball bat, so swinging one in defense is out.) And when I think about it now, the fear returns, viscerally. Sweaty palms, swallow breathing, and a sense of foreboding. I start to dread future trips to parking garages. I wonder if I should re-up self-defense classes.

The zombie apocalypse appeared as a likelihood rather than fantasy I could dismiss handily, and instantly, I regretted my lack of attention, preparation, and survival skills. (I also can't render pig fat into gasoline.)

In that stairwell, I felt the terror that many Americans

feel today, and even spend part of their lives preparing for. My fear, then, was far from unique.

From the Centers for Disease Control and Prevention's emergency preparedness campaign to a Miami man who supposedly consumed the flesh of his victim to groups of Americans who sacrifice time and money to prepare for the zombie apocalypse, Americans both fear and desire the arrival of *real* zombies. They want movie monsters to be a threat to our shared world. Some eagerly anticipate this end-of-the-world scenario by stockpiling food and weapons. They plan for its inevitability. Some search for signs, clues even, of zombification and conspiracy theories. Others prepare by purchasing ammunition marketed specifically for zombie killing or shooting at 3D zombie targets that ooze and come apart every time they are hit. The zombie apocalypse, for these Americans, is not just a fiction, but a potential outcome for which all of us should prepare.

Zombies, they think, are coming, so the time to get ready is now.

Before we move further, you should know—if you haven't guessed already—that I am nowhere near prepared for any form of doomsday, much less zombies ending our world. I will surely be one of the first casualties of the dystopian world yet to come.

More than that, I am not *even* a fan of zombies. Honestly, I don't like them much at all. What I am is a writer and scholar of American religions and popular culture, and I spend much of my time researching and writing apocalypses, so the popularity of the zombie apocalypses both right now and in the recent past intrigues me. I want to know why the zombie apocalypse fascinates Americans, so I started paying attention to these monsters and their prevalence in pop culture. I've lost count of the amount of times I've watched *Zombieland* (2009), which is likely my favorite undead film with *Warm Bodies* (2013) a close second place. Alongside millions of other Americans, I used to regularly tune into AMC's *The Walking Dead* (2010-present), and I can discuss George Romero's long-standing contributions and legacy to zombie cinema, if you ask nicely. I have read more novels about zombies than I will admit aloud.

Simply put, I have zombies on the brain. My sudden panicked moment in a parking garage about my own demise could be explained away by my hours upon hours of exposure to what I call *zombie media*, all those the novels, movies, TV shows, apps, memes, and video games that center on this monster.

Unsurprisingly, my dreamscape is often zombified too. I wake up soaked in sweat and shaky from vivid nightmares in which the dead rise. Night after night, I battle resurrected corpses and die, painfully and slowly. Or worse, I survive the monsters but lose those I love most to the shambling horde. I never get to say goodbye, and the overwhelming grief at their loss follows me after I wake up and through my day. Or much worse, I watch them transform into the ravenous undead who no longer recognize me as mother, partner, sister, daughter, or friend. Instead, they hunt me down because I only matter to them as a possible meal. The horror of their transformation startles me from sleep and makes me too upset to even try to return to sleep for fear of what my next nightmare might bring.

Still, that vision of my death by monsters lingers with me, which continues to surprise me.

After all, if anyone should know better about the fantasy, or unreality, of zombies, *it's me*. The walking dead only exist in television, film, fiction, and video games, not in daily life. *Monsters are make-believe*, I remind myself in my daughter's singsong voice, *they aren't real*. I do know better. And yet, *and yet*, for the briefest of moments, I believed that zombies could be stalking me in a dark garage or lying in wait at the bottom of a stairwell. Once again, my overactive imagination got the best of me (which it is already apt to do). I could—and maybe should—shrug this off as an anomaly. This one time, I let fantasy merge with my reality. We all have this happen sometimes, don't we? I still wonder why it happened to me.

Zombies aren't real. I know better. But the questions continue to echo in my head: *Are they?*

While walking corpses might not be taking over our planet as I write, the zombie apocalypse as a fictional genre has never been so popular. Zombies are *all over the place*. They are the cultural monsters of the moment, having replaced vampires, werewolves, aliens, and other monsters as the nightmare *du jour*. According to cultural critic Lev Grossman, "once you start looking, you see them everywhere."[2] They shamble and moan in every nook and cranny of American pop culture, antagonizing, maiming, and killing humans. Writing in 2013 for *The Globe and Mail*, media critic and journalist Geoff Pevere noted:

> The zombie apocalypse is real. Maybe not in the sense of re-animated flesh-eating corpses trudging down your street, but definitely in the pop-culture sense. We're being eaten alive by the damned things, and we love it.

They eat us, and, ironically, we consume them too, especially when they bring about doomsday. Zombies emerge again and again as the reason for the end of the world. Often, this cataclysm is visualized as the end of America as we know it now, it's the midwife for a mangled society of human survivors facing not only the menacing undead but also the danger and violence of fellow humans. Pevere continued that these monsters are "the perfect horror-movie metaphor" for the twentieth and twenty-first centuries, "the age of the alienated mass."[3] And he's right. They are a metaphor that just won't stop. They can't stay dead. And they resonated with us in years past and continue to resonate.

A Fox station in Tampa Bay, FL noted that the "whole world seemed zombie crazy."[4] A statement, unfortunately marked by ableism, points to a larger truth about the presence and popularity of zombies. They just won't go away because Americans still love them. We continue to live in what political scientist Daniel W. Drezner described as the "zombie boom" in 2010.[5] (Less generously, the Associated Press wondered if these monsters appear now as our "unhealthy obsessions with death and decay."[6] Zombie obsession makes mass interest in zombies appear pathological. A moralizing judgment rather than analysis about their popularity and prevalence.)

Zombies were and are mainstream staples. And ten years later, in 2020, the living dead just won't seem to go away, and in fact, they continue to thrive in American pop culture.

Let's take a look at what this zombie boom includes. *The Walking Dead* has broken records for cable television network viewership. As of 2017, it was the highest-rated show on television, and it is the only drama to "hold the top spot in adults 18-49 for five years in a row."[7] (However, the ratings of the ninth season were at an all-time low). The film adaptation of Max Brook's *World War Z* (2006) hit the big screen in 2013. Brad Pitt battled fast-moving zombies while jetting around the world for a cure for the zombie plague, and the film raked in $540 million worldwide. Shelves of local bookstores groan under the weight of the many books on zombies from science fiction and horror to romance to middle grade and young adult fiction.

Zombies additionally show up in graphic novels, comics, music (from Michael Jackson's epic "Thriller" music video and a zombified Taylor Swift in her "Look What You Made Me Do" video to band names like White Zombie and Zombie Apocalypse), social media, video games, apparel, bumper stickers, posters, and toys. Zombies "walk" in cities all over the U.S., and hacked road signs warn of their presence at construction zones and closed roads as well as the occasional rogue emergency alert.

These monsters also emerge as fodder for parody, including *Pat the Zombie* (2011), a mash-up of zombies and the popular children's book, *Pat the Bunny* (1940); the bestselling hybrid of Jane Austen and zombie hunting, *Pride and Prejudice and Zombies* (2009); and Greg Stones' *Zombies Hate Stuff* (2012), a collection of water colors depicting all the things zombies hate, including kittens, ninjas, disrespect, unicorns, and clowns. Runners have dodged zombies in 5K fun runs. College students equipped with Nerf guns have played Humans versus Zombies on their university campuses. Amusement parks, like Universal Studios, have incorporated the shambling horde into their Halloween events.

And a fair number of trick-or-treaters have arrived at my door every October 31st dressed as gruesome zombies with gray face paint and fake blood dripping down their chins, zombified princesses complete with fancy dresses, tiaras, and deep black circles under their eyes, or even zombie cheerleaders replete with skirt, pom poms, and a tendency to eat brains. (I have even done the make-up for these types of small zombies, once or twice.)

Zombies truly are everywhere.

In 2011, *24/7 Wall Street* estimated that the zombie economy was an over five-billion-dollar industry when combining television, book, film, merchandise, and video game revenues. Movies alone make up $2.5 billion. Additionally, it's likely the $5.74 billion that zombies bring into the economy is actually a low-ball estimate with *24/7 Wall Street* emphasizing that "this tab is grossly undercalculated in each category."[8] Zombies are not only the monsters of our moment, but also major money makers too. They are popular, profitable, and unavoidable.

One of the reasons I started researching zombies and later the zombie apocalypse was because of the sheer abundance of zombies. These monsters are ever-present, and their continued existence signals something important about America in the early twenty-first century. Zombies, after all, become metaphors for anything from consumerism and class warfare to terrorism and mindless politics/politicians to epidemics and fear of the government to smartphone users and even fear of our neighbors. And they hang around because of their metaphorical potential to stand in for so many things that concern us now. There's something about them that has reverberated starting almost two decades ago, unsurprisingly after 9/11, and continues to echo now.

Zombies do cultural work like all other monsters do. And according to Jeffrey Jerome Cohen, "We live in a time of monsters."[9] He was writing in the 1990s, but his insight remains timely. We continue to inhabit a time of monsters. Monsters never seem to go away; they hang around and make sure we pay attention to them. In *Monster Theory: Reading Culture*, Cohen argues that the monster is "an embodiment of a certain cultural moment" and comes to represent our fears, desires, anxieties, and fantasies.[10] Monsters reveal things that we maybe don't want them to. They show us what concerns us. They show us what appeals to us. They remind us of what we fear. They are always a reflection of the culture that births them.

And right now, we inhabit the time of a particular monster who resurrects, shambles, and moans. The zombie won't go away until we listen to the story, or stories, that it wants to tell us about us. It won't go away until we truly pay attention and reckon with what the zombie shows us about our culture. We also have to figure out what it embodies. It's here to stay, presenting what we fear and desire until new fears and desires take their place.

While I was looking at zombies and what they might reveal about America, something else caught my attention and I decided to follow where it went. What really stuck out to me was all the people who described the zombie apocalypse, a fictional event, as an *actual possibility*.

I first encountered this sensibility from my students. I used to teach a course called The Apocalypse in American Culture that covered the different types of doomsday that Americans prophesied, believed in, and hoped for. In papers for that class, some students assured me that *when* the zombie apocalypse occurred, they would be ready. Moreover, in their class evaluations, they suggested that my class helped them prepare for this particular end of the world scenario. I remain doubtful that my class actually helped them with emergency preparedness in general or monsters in particular. Being able to critically analyze narratives will not save you from a monster. Instead, it might make you monster food.

Their claims of reality at first surprised, then amused, and then finally shocked me. What did they mean by *when*? Why not the less committed *if*? I could not understand how a fictional end might appear possible or desirable. The apocalypse is never a happy ending; it's a crisis to be avoided at all costs. How did zombies shift from fantasy to probability? Why might doomsday at the hands and teeth of monsters appeal to some Americans? Or, the more important question, why did they want zombies to be *real*?

A monster at your doorstep brings horror, not hope. Perhaps, I underestimated the power of fiction and fantasy to shape reality. Perhaps, the line between what's real and what we believe is not is more porous that we claim it is. Maybe the students were teasing me because they thought I was an easy mark. Maybe I misunderstood their *when*. Maybe the fictional apocalypse is more fun to ponder than actual disasters and what we stand to lose. Maybe zombies causing an apocalypse seems easier to manage than the intricacies and complexities of our world.

INTRODUCTION: "MOMMY, ZOMBIES AREN'T REAL."

The more I explored the fantasy of the zombie apocalypse in popular culture, the more I confronted the ways in which people make the zombie apocalypse into a potential reality. Many Americans eagerly await the zombies, while others fear the end of the world as we know it. Cracked.com notes that zombies are possibly the coolest way for the world to end when one considers the other options, like plagues, meteors, or other natural disasters.[11]

The zombie apocalypse, my students assured me, would be *awesome*. A world with no rules, no government, and no infrastructure appealed to them. They readied themselves for the monsters by strategizing about how to survive and making plans. And yet, my students were not alone. This desire for the zombie apocalypse goes beyond my students' claims and the humor of Cracked.com—some Americans not only believe that zombies will end the world, but they eagerly prepare for this end-times vision.

They materialize this form of doomsday with every bit of preparation, every purchase of guns and ammo, and every strategy session on how to survive. And others do, too, when using the zombie apocalypse for hurricane preparedness campaigns, tactical training for military and civilians, and when relying on the narratives of the genre to report news events.

People believe in the zombie apocalypse and acting on those beliefs makes it real.

And yet, those who want the zombie apocalypse are not an anomaly. Many Americans want the end of the world as we know it—not just by monsters—and they are more than fine with where that kind of catastrophe would lead. (For the record, I am not.) They are eager for an end and what might follow.

Before we can get to the reality of zombies and their doomsdays, we have to consider the American fascination and attachment to apocalypses more generally. The continuing desire for the world to end, both past and present, is not going away any time soon. It's time to consider the apocalypse, the people who want it to happen, and the stakes for all of us in the hope for doomsday of any kind.

2

"APOCALYPSE OBSESSION."

Apocalypticism's Past and Present

The end of the world is always and never near—and it matters that we understand why.
—Kelly J. Murphy[1]

In 2012, CNN journalist Nicole Saidi wrote about the popular and "kind of exciting" appeal of apocalypticism.[2] That year, we were sort of in an apocalyptic moment, or at least, what appeared to be one. According to some, there was a forthcoming end to the world because of the end of the Mayan calendar on December 21, 2012. (Some capitalized on this concern over cataclysm by writing books or appearing on TV shows to tell what they thought we should know). Combined with the concern over the Mayan calendar, others suggested a large planet might crash into Earth, a planet that no one had ever documented as even existing.

Scientists at NASA released a video to debunk the claims about the "Mayan apocalypse" and pointed out that this calendar's end was just like any other. It was a regular shift from one year to the next, just like other years in our modern calendar. They year 2012 would pass by just like all the years preceding it. Also, NASA wanted us to know that there was no giant planet that would crush us into oblivion. Astronomers would have probably given us a heads up if that kind of event was going to happen.[3]

And in 2012, it wasn't just the Mayan calendar drumming up visions of the end. The apocalypse was everywhere you looked: television, film, social media, and news coverage. Harold Camping of Family Radio gained notoriety when he predicted the end of the world in 2011. Family Radio was a California-based ministry, which caught public attention when they sponsored 1200 billboards in 2010 and 2011 to warn Americans that Judgment Day was upon us.[4] When the world's end didn't happen in 2011, Camping pushed his prediction back to 2012. The apocalypse proved again to be a no show.

The *Left Behind* series (1995–2007), co-authored by Tim LaHaye and Jerry Jenkins, sold over 80 million copies, as of 2016. The series detailed a ragtag group of people left behind after their version of the Rapture, the ascension of true believers to Heaven before the Second Coming of Christ. The books showed what the end times might be: a lot of violence, punishment, blood and gore, and the arrival of a vengeful Jesus ready to judge those who weren't believers. They garnered their place as fixtures in major bookstores shelved with the rest of Christian fiction.

The post-apocalyptic *Hunger Games* trilogy (2008-2010) fascinated readers and the film, released in March of 2012, interested filmgoers, too. The first film made over $694 million at the box office. (My dad, for instance, loved the first film and impatiently waited for the others to follow.) In 2011, National Geographic aired "Doomsday Preppers," a show documenting various people preparing for all kinds of disasters. It became the channel's most watched show. In film, actor Will Smith repeatedly saved the world from various threats from the 1990s and 2000s through the 2012 release of *Men in Black 3*. In previous years, he fought off aliens multiple times, kept robots from taking over, and faced off against zombie-like vampires in a post-apocalyptic U.S. in *I Am Legend* (2007).

Adding up all of these with the cottage industry that sprang up around the Mayan calendar, it did appear that apocalypticism was having a bit of a moment in 2012. The whole year, it seemed, had an apocalyptic mood.

Relying on Google Trends, Saidi reported for CNN that web searches for "zombies" topped the other "apocalypse-oriented terms" while "end of the world" peaked when paired with zombies. "Doomsday," however, was not the most popular search term. It's an old-fashioned word for the apocalypse, which isn't used as much anymore, so there's no surprise that it didn't appear as often in searches.

For Saidi, this searching for the end of the world became an "apocalypse obsession," a possibly pathological attention to all things end-times.[5] We couldn't just be interested in apocalypticism because it was unavoidable; we had to be obsessed, which suggested that there was something wrong with anyone who believed one of these end of the world scenarios as well as those of us who paid attention to it. Americans appeared largely apocalyptic, which seemed to signal that many Americans hoped for bad endings awaiting us in the future, and it appeared to be a new "obsession" that required attention and a headline.

Friends began jokingly asking me for my professional opinion about what might end us, and I refused to comment. I am not a doomsday prophet. I doubt I ever will be.

While Saidi is right that Americans seemed "obsessed" with the apocalypse in 2012—and even now, eight years later, the so-called obsession hasn't abated—

it's a mistake to understand apocalypticism as only a late twentieth and early twenty-first century phenomenon. Americans did not just discover the apocalypse in the 2010s. It's not new, and it's easy to find instances of apocalyptic thinking and beliefs in recent history.

For instance, think back to the panic around the Y2K bug, a problem in coding—over the calendar switch to January 1, 2000. (What is it with calendars?) This bug was predicted to have calamitous effects because folks thought that it could, maybe, crash computer systems all over the world. People feared that it would affect banks, transportation, and power plants, especially nuclear power plants. Things could have gone awry in such a way that we would all find the world changed. We would all be impacted because computers are essential to how our world runs. Our dependence on computers is complete and to lose them would have been a serious blow to our everyday lives. The combination of the computer bug and the coming of a new millennium (year 2000) led some folks to predict the world would end on Jan. 1, 2000. The new year could bring about a new world order, and some people began to store food and prepare for our possible demise.

I remember the media attention and fears surrounding the Y2K bug. At the end of 1999, I was nineteen years old and a know-it-all, who was not quite convinced that Dec. 31, 1999 would be our last day of the world that we inhabited together. I doubted the beginning of the end would simply happen when the clock struck midnight and new year dawned. How could a bug in code—something I imagined to be small but wasn't—cause a real doomsday? I had confidence in computer programmers to handle the problem; they could manage to avert disaster, right? One of my friends, my grudging boyfriend (studying computer science at a university), and I kind of wanted to see what would happen. We stayed up until midnight on New Year's Eve, sitting outside in the dark in rural north Florida, ready to be witnesses to an unprecedented transformation. The hours ticked by, and we waited.

Midnight came and went, and nothing happened. We wasted our time and lost sleep over the unremarkable shift from one year to the next. I'll admit that I was mildly disappointed (teenagers, man) that there was no end in sight; all that hype, hand-wringing, and fear was for nothing because the world remained standing, unfazed by our human predictions and prophecies.

But mostly I was relieved that nothing had happened. I wasn't ready for the end of the world as I knew it, and I definitely wasn't prepared for it. I was glad our world was resilient enough to pass through a potential end-times unscathed. It took the efforts of many, many programmers to avert disaster. I was glad that a computer glitch couldn't destroy our society and those fragile bonds that hold us together. I was glad to have survived, even as I started to wonder about those who believed that the world could bite the dust so suddenly and completely.

The Y2K bug fizzled, but other apocalypses quickly took its place. Some Americans looked forward to the end again and again. And they weren't alone, or unique.

The apocalypse is a part of not only the recent past but also part of our history. It clearly didn't come into existence in 2012. Instead, it's a longstanding component of American culture and history. Americans, both past and present, looked and still look for signs of the end times. They predicted and still predict the end. They prepared and continue to prepare, even now, for what might come after.

In the seventeenth century, Puritan ministers wrote jeremiads that catalogued the potential destruction of the world. Revivalists proclaimed that awakenings were clearly signs of divine providence in the eighteenth century. In the lead-up to the Civil War, enslaved Black people and white masters saw slavery as either an evil corruption of the world or a new path to a civilization. Mormons imagined themselves as a chosen people living in the latter days. Millerites believed the end would arrive in 1844 and experienced painful disappointments, the Great Disappointment actually, when the date came and went without the foretold apocalypse occurring. At the end of the nineteenth century, Lakota Ghost Dancers hoped for a new world free from white colonialism. Pentecostals, Black and white, saw speaking in tongues as a divine sign signaling the end of days. After World War II, the nuclear bomb became a gruesome sign of how all humanity could be easily destroyed, a sign that the end was closer than we might want to think.

Now, environmentalists project a secular apocalypse involving global warming, which we now label climate change to show the breadth of the dangers that await us when the temperature of the earth's atmosphere rises. Their predictions are met by recent, terrifying studies about the fate of our planet.

In January of 2019, the Bulletin of the Atomic Scientists kept the Doomsday Clock at two minutes to midnight, which is a bad sign. Created in 1945, the Clock is a symbol of how close we are to human extinction and the risks that we face: political, environmental, technological, and nuclear. The online magazine *Vox* tells us that we should be "worried." The Doomsday Clock's time symbolizes our proximity to catastrophe. And right now, Jerry Brown, chair of the Bulletin and a former governor of California, noted, "We're playing Russian roulette with humanity."[6] The minute hand, hovering so close to midnight, shows us that the world can end, without interventions. The Bulletin lists all the threats to humanity. The Clock offers a message that we should worry about and fear for the future because of all the threats we face. It's another message about how close the apocalypse might be. It's another doomsday prophecy, but this time, issued by scientists and not prophets. (And yet, its message is more authentic and worrisome than the rest.)

Currently, the Covid-19 pandemic makes it feel like we are hovering near apocalypse as it ravages the globe. People are dying, and the world feels as if it is on fire, a fire that we can't seem to put out. The end feels nearer and more pressing. As of May 2020, the clock is set at one hundred seconds to midnight. We're now seconds rather than minutes away from catastrophe.

The end is near, the end is near, the end is near.

This emerges as a common refrain. It resonates loudly through our past into the present, a warning about our lack of a future.

A long line of Americans stated, proclaimed, shouted, cajoled, argued, hoped, wished, and desired the end of the world because they all wanted to play a part in the final days. They all wanted to be a starring role in a world at its end or at least be a supporting character, so they would be right about what happens next. Harold Camping, the focus on the Mayan calendar, the Y2K bug, and others are part of a larger trend, not a recent "obsession" with end times.

Apocalypticism is neither an outlier nor an oddity.

The apocalypse is a defining feature of the nation, not some glitch that pops up now and again to draw our attention.

And yet, there remains a real reticence among scholars, journalists, and pundits to admit that predictions of the end-times and desire for a new, different world created after disaster might be more common that they are comfortable with. This isn't really shocking. Who would want to acknowledge that apocalypticism defines us past and present? Attention to doomsday beliefs and practices suggests that the story we tell of American progress and democracy is not anywhere near the whole story of America's past or present. At best, it's a partial one that tells a more comfortable story about our past than we need or deserve. At worst, it's a story that purposefully hides the conflict, violence, and brutality that make up American history. It's a dodge, not the truth.

To take the prevalence of apocalypticism seriously requires taking a hard look at our culture (and history) to evaluate what we really see. It's likely we will not like what we find and will try to avoid it. Unfortunately, what this means is that scholarship and news coverage of doomsday beliefs and believers often try to paint apocalypticism as strange, bizarre, inconsequential—tangential at best, or fringe at the worst. It emerges as marginal beliefs and practices of a marginal few, who can be discounted with ease by scholars and journalists. Those who believe in doomsday don't really matter, they contend, so they get dismissed.

Many, in academia and in public, might hope and proclaim that apocalypticism is only a disturbing "obsession" or "creed for cranks." [7] There's a problem with this approach because apocalypticism is anything but marginal.

Take for instance results from several polls from the last ten years that ask questions about the end. In a 2010 Telegraph poll, 41% of Americans polled believed Jesus would return in the next 40 years. A 2011 Public Religion Research Institute poll of white evangelicals documented that 67% thought that they were currently living in the end times. The Summer 2013 OmniPoll found that 41% of adults in the U.S., and 77% of evangelicals, also thought all of us were living through the end times right now.[8] (Even if the rest of us didn't know it.) A YouGov Poll from 2015 found that 1/3 of the Americans surveyed rated an "apocalyptic disaster" as somewhat to very likely. Another survey (also from 2015) of folks in the U.S., Canada, Australia, and the United Kingdom found that 54% thought there was at least a 50% risk "that our way of life will end in the next 100 years."[9] The Americans surveyed—perhaps not surprisingly—were the most pessimistic about the fate of our future existence.

The concern for the end of the world, however, doesn't translate into getting prepared for its occurrence. Vox reports that around two-thirds of Americans surveyed admitted that they had "given little or no thought to preparing for the apocalypse."[10] The apocalypse might be happening, but most Americans aren't quite rushing into doomsday prep. Perhaps preparation isn't necessary when you already think we are living through the end times right *now*.

So, despite its marginalization and pathologization in news coverage, this longing for doomsday is not just for cranks or an easily dismissed few. Americans believe in the end and answer questions about it in surveys. It's commonplace and abundant. It's popular and prevalent. It's not marginal, even if that would make us rest easier. We can't be quick to dismiss its place in our culture. Americans promote, consume, and affirm these catastrophic visions over and over again.

Graphic imaginings of ends, then, are as American as apple pie. Religious and not-so-religious Americans yearn for a variety of apocalypses to critique, reform and revolutionize American society. By engaging this desire for the end, the darker side of American life appears starkly against American claims for progress, religious freedom, diversity, and pluralism. Apocalypticism, with its melding of dystopian and utopian impulses, emerges as a mechanism both of social vision and critique. Some

Americans long for a world that is anything but this one. Some want to guarantee that the end happens. Some prepare for it with glee or fatalism, or a heady combination of both.

While apocalypticism tends to be most commonly understood as a catastrophic end-of-the-world scenario, the term's original meaning isn't tied to disaster or catastrophe. Those definitions came later and overshadowed its origins. Apocalypse comes from the Greek root word *apocalypsis,* which can mean either revelation or unveiling.[11] A revelation can be that sudden, surprising fact that makes you realize something important. Or something about the world is unveiled— our vision moves from obscured to clear—which means you can never see the world as it was before. The veil falls away from us, and we can have knowledge that we didn't even want. In a religious setting, revelation can be something that a supernatural or divine force discloses to humans, knowledge granted that we didn't have access to until now.

Apocalypses that we imagine, then, reveal something to us about both our world and ourselves; they show us things we might not know—or might not want to face. They also show us things about our world that demonstrate that what we might want our world to be is not necessarily what *it is.* Revelation discloses. It leaves us changed. It marks a before and an after, and it is impossible to go back to before. We're stuck with what we now know.

So, it is interesting that a word that first meant "unveiling" now is synonymous with the calamitous end of the world. Apocalypses now appear as visions that chart the end of the current world and the beginning of a new one. Apocalypticism is a form of millennialism. This term has its roots in the word "millennium," a one-thousand-year period. Millennialism, however, is concerned with more than the passage of a certain amount of time, and it reflects the desire for and belief in a particular type of millennium, a period of one thousand years of peace that might occur either before or after the end of the world as we know it.

Religious studies scholar Shawn Landes describes the "profoundly subversive notion" that our current world "is not the natural world" because something more authentic is on the horizon.[12] Political scientist Michael Barkun describes these expectations of the millennium as "the sense of belief that the existing order will disappear" followed by "a world free of conflict and suffering."[13] There's another world waiting for us—better than the one we live in now—that only requires the end of our world to arrive. (Though there are some versions of millennialism that are more progressive and assume that humans will bring about one thousand years of peace before the world's end. They are not the people this book documents.)

Now, there's a tentative optimism in millennialism about how the future might be better than our present. This recreated world awaits us—a world that is separate from the strife, chaos, and violence that we confront now. All our social problems get left behind; nothing bad follows us forward. Peace is what we'll find. And yet, we can only have the future we want if we are willing to sacrifice the present. We can only start all over once the old order no longer exists. The temptation to wipe the slate clean defines millennialism. If we could only start again, our lives would be improved. (But would they?)

Apocalypticism, then, is a particular type of millennialism, which scholar Catherine Wessinger describes as "catastrophic." It's defined by pessimism about our history, our current society, and the fate of our world.[14] The optimism is muted, or in some cases, completely gone. The current world appears so corrupt and terrible that the only way to fix it is through destroying it; there's no redemption available for our present. The world gets annihilated so we can start over and hopefully (but maybe not) build a better and brighter world. Often, catastrophic millennialism assumes that some divine force brings about the millennium, not humans, because we need outside help for anything to change. Destruction, often by divine intervention, is the only means to bring about the social change that some think we desperately need.

In much of American history, apocalypses have tended to be religious, but they can also be secular, like those environmental doomsday scenarios discussed earlier in this chapter. Folklorist Daniel Wojcik argues that secular apocalypses are a more recent phenomenon than the more common religious ones. After World War II, nuclear weapons changed the understanding of the world. When the United States dropped atom bombs on Hiroshima and Nagasaki in August of 1945, the mushroom clouds, the total devastation of the cities, and the remarkable loss of life became the signs of a new era—a decidedly more terrifying one.

When I was in high school in the 1990s, my history teacher made us watch a documentary about the bombs and their aftermath in both cities, and I have never forgotten the graphic images of the dead and the wounds and scars that marked survivors' bodies. I gained a sense of the harrowing potential of these weapons to harm, maim, and kill because it was obvious in each grainy image that skirted across the screen. The damage that they wrought was hard to process and overwhelming. I was not the only one who started crying.

By the time class ended, I was numb. And I also realized the futility of drills that my elementary school forced us through to prepare us for a nuclear attack.

Hiding under our desks wouldn't help us survive; nothing would. From one minute to the next, we wouldn't exist. We would be dead, no matter what drill we practiced.

Like Americans from generations before me, I learned that nuclear weapons could not only end wars but also bring about the total annihilation of humanity. They could end us with an ease that remains terrifying and disturbing. The use of nuclear weapons in World War II fundamentally changed how Americans understood *how* our world might end. Here was a terrifying new scenario, shorn of divine intervention, which suggested the future was not guaranteed as we had come to imagine. The advent and use of nuclear weapons birthed secular apocalypticism, which was steeped in fatalism for our future. It would be a bleak one at best—at worst, it would be one that never happened. Any tentative optimism about a new world faded fast. What might happen next was no longer a comforting vision of years and years of peace, but the likelihood of human extinction.

And now, Americans still fear nuclear war and its destructive potential. A YouGov poll from 2015 found that 28% of Americans surveyed believed that nuclear war would be the "most likely cause of the apocalypse."[15] Nuclear weapons give humans the ability to destroy all on a grand scale. It becomes too easy to wipe out humanity completely. It becomes too easy to leave the world in ruins. While some forms of the apocalypse offered a chance at something better than we have now, the threat of nuclear weapons meant there was no longer a chance at redemption awaiting us in the world's ashes, or even hope for divine intercession to save us. The divine, in all of its shapes and forms, no longer cared about us. So the future was dim and frightening. Things could only get worse.

Catastrophe and destruction became both means and ends. The world would surely be destroyed, and destruction would be all that remained. And it was all our own fault. Secular doomsday squarely rested all the blame on our shoulders; our actions would bring about our own extinction. Humans were clearly terrible creatures in a fallen world. All we could do was break our world—not refashion it.

The end appeared not only near but also certain, fated even.[16] Humans would manage to end one another. We wouldn't be able to stop ourselves. We couldn't even if we tried.

Our actions no longer mattered because we couldn't prevent the inevitable annihilation. There was nothing we could do, so why try? The world is a goner, and secular apocalypticism attempts to force us to recognize our own futility and embrace fatalism. The future was already threatened by constant peril, and we knew how the story, our story, would end. There was finality here that hadn't quite existed before. The advent and use of nuclear weapons changed how we understood the world around us and how we understood ourselves. Human survival was no longer expected. No future loomed before us because we had none. We were just waiting for that end to actually occur.

Of course, this newer secular form of apocalypticism didn't mean that religious apocalypticism disappeared. It continued to exist, and secular apocalypticism influenced its religious cousin. Religious apocalypticism took a bleaker turn too, though the possibility of divine reckoning and a remaking of the world offered a hint of a future. So, the boundaries between religious and secular apocalypses are not as clearly marked as one might imagine; they are more blurry than distinct. They continue to inform one another. They change one another. They continue to exist side-by-side, sometimes, offering very similar visions of a desolate future and humanity's inability to be redeemed. They sound the same warnings, even as they speak them differently.

Apocalypticisms, religious and secular, are more common than you may think. They surround us; we can't get away from them.

Scholar of English and American studies Lee Quinby notes that the various forms of apocalypticism contain common traits: prophecy, lament, prophets, skeptics, elect, dystopia, fatalism, utopia, dualism, death, destruction, catastrophe, and eventual justice. Destruction remains the preferred method of social recreation and revolution. And yet, there's more to them than what first appears. They are about doomsday, but not solely. We make a mistake if we focus solely on apocalypticism as a variety of end-times scenarios that people believe, enact, and embody. Scholars Kathleen Stewart and Susan Harding describe apocalypticism as a *mode* that not only draws our attention but also offers us knowledge about our world. Apocalyptic attention and knowing, then, have come to "structure modern American life." It can't be limited to some so-called strange beliefs or theologies, people who prophesied the end, or ideas that only inhabit the margins of American culture. It is more expansive and influential.

They write that apocalypticism evokes "horror and hope, nightmare and dream, destruction and creation, dystopia and utopia."[17] It's a feeling and a mood. It's a vision that creates and destroys. It's imagining a world of ruins or of peace. More than that, the apocalyptic comes to define how Americans interpret our nation and the world around us. It becomes a lens to explain what's happening in our world, our interactions with all the people in it, and how we orient ourselves in our day-to-day lives. The apocalyptic not only inhabits our culture but also our minds. We think, experience, interact, and feel through this mode.

The danger of the apocalyptic mode, particularly after World War II, is its fatalism. *Ours is a world beyond saving*, the apocalyptic tells us, *so why try?*

Fatalism becomes accepted truth rather than a notion that is up for debate or refusal. We don't have to act to change the inevitable annihilation that follows.[18] We are expected not to. We might be actively encouraged to not challenge the status quo. The apocalyptic can make us complacent, but that is not all it does.

According to Quinby, the power of the apocalyptic is that it also helps us make meaning in our lives. The apocalyptic, she writes, has "rules and conventions for establishing meaning, designating the true from the false, empowering certain speakers and writers and disqualifying others."[19] The apocalyptic helps us clarify our world by simplifying the nuance and complexity. It flattens and smoothes over ambiguity and ambivalence. There's only true and false, and nothing in between. There are only those we can trust and those we can't. There are only those we listen to and those we don't. Our interactions with the world marked by unwavering certainty about the rightness of our positions and the wrongness of all others. The apocalyptic offers meaning about our world that makes life appear simpler than it is. The messiness of life is washed away by following the rules of the apocalyptic and seeing where they lead. Complexity is sacrificed for clarity.

What worries Quinby (and arguably should worry us, too) about this type of meaning-making is that apocalypticism delays our ethical wranglings about what's happening now—because nothing matters right now if a new, better world awaits us or if the future doesn't even exist. Why care about the present and its injustices when the better future awaits? Why care about justice at all if the new beginning you really want is so close? Why worry about *the now*? Why act when you can just wait patiently for all the problems of the present to be instantly fixed in the future? Or why care about anything if the world's days are numbered? Why should we care at all? Ethics goes by the wayside because *what comes next* matters more than the injustices that exist right now.

Even if that new world is born through violence and devastation, it doesn't matter if we get the future we want.[20] Our ends are always seemingly more important than our means. Our future always more important than the here and now, even if we might not have that future we're looking forward to. The present always seems irreparable and irredeemable. *The now* is perpetually disappointing.

Rather than solely theologies or beliefs, apocalypticism is a system of interpretation as well as power relations. It's indebted to a negative view of humans as inherently violent, selfish, and destructive. It offers up nostalgia for a fabled past where things made sense and a future where they might again. It contains countless laments about *the now* and the supposed chaos of our present. It entails a profound yearning for a future society created amidst the ruins of our current world. It's a reset to our world that most of us won't survive. It's a reset that some think we need no matter how steep the consequences or the body count.

Americans have embraced apocalypticism for centuries, and they have wanted the world to end in a variety of ways in a variety of times and places. The types of doomsday abound; there are so many ways to get to the end.

But, what Stewart, Harding, and Quinby point out is that apocalypticism is also a way to inhabit the world; it's a worldview that suggests a particular type of engagement with the present that is more concerned with the future. Visions of the end impact how Americans interact in our day-to-day lives, politics, and culture. Yes, Americans do imagine and have imagined cataclysmic ends to both the nation and the larger world, in which annihilation becomes the required predecessor to a better world. (Though, the future being brighter seems to be less guaranteed or possible now. Or does it? I wouldn't rush to judgment.)

Sometimes, the world they yearn for is not better, but worse than our present, like an apocalypse in which zombies roam and humans become prey. It's fatalistic and awful. It's a world in ruins. These impulses, dystopian and (less and less) utopian, become inseparable in every marked date and failed prophecy.[21] Some Americans want an end because they imagine an end is the only way to move forward. The possibility of the apocalypse shapes how they view our shared world, and this, I would argue, is not good for any of us.

Often, the end feels easier than *the now*. In *Hope in the Dark*, Rebecca Solnit writes: "People have always been good at imagining the end of the world, which is much easier to picture than the strange sidelong paths of change in a world without end."[22] The only time a better future appears—if it appears at all—is after our current world is destroyed. The social vision of that better future is built upon devastation, ruin, and a massive loss of life. A reset is more desirable than doing the hard work to save our current world. Calling it quits also offers absolution from responsibility.

Quit on the world, I guess, before the world can quit on you.

Our preferred apocalypses, then, come to define us and affect what we think and how we act. If the world is about to end, what do you do? Maybe nothing. Maybe something. It depends on how you think it will all end and whether you think what you do will even matter.

Those preferred ends reveal what we value and what we don't, who we care about and who we ignore, and what we will do and how we refuse to act. They are commentary not only on the moments we inhabit together right now, but also on who we are and what kind of people we yearn to be. Apocalypses contain our hopes and fears bundled together in our vision of a world on a fast-approaching deadline.

What I keep coming back to with apocalypticism is the assumption that the world must end, often violently, if it is ever to be saved (or maybe, not saved at all). That the world must end is a fact that those who wait for the end accept as necessary truth, the inevitable path that we can't help but trod. It haunts me that Americans, past and present, think our world is beyond saving. That our world is a goner because it can't be changed through ordinary means or social action. That nothing we can do can change our terrible fate. That the future is bleak and that's acceptable, normal even. That we might be facing down annihilation, but maybe that's all we can expect.

The reset button is tempting, oh-so-tempting. And on bad days when I scroll through the news and see political corruption, mass shootings, children being separated from their families at the U.S.-Mexico border, civil rights being eroded, and the deliberate political mismanagement of the Covid-19 pandemic, I feel this temptation viscerally. I can see the appeal in letting everything burn. When the flames subside and ash covers the ground, we can start over and create a world not plagued by our current problems.

Let it burn, I think, *how could what comes next be worse?*

And yet, it could be worse. It can always be worse. Fatalism is good at dwelling in the terrible while ignoring the good. Because while these injustices overwhelm me, and maybe you too, there's also activism and activists working hard to make the present and future more just and sustainable for all of us. They have hope for both *the now* and *the what comes next*, so I also resist the temptation of the reset, even as I still feel it, because the reset won't be neutral. It will have grave effects on some and not others, so it's crucial to know what that suggested reset might entail, what it is supposed to bring about, and who it targets. A reset also suggests that our present is too far gone, which I refuse to believe, even as others continue to.

Apocalypticism, then, was never only about a set of doomsday scenarios but about how we decide to approach the world and all of us who inhabit it. The apocalyptic is a worldview that brings with it consequences. So, to examine American apocalypticism, then, is to examine what matters and doesn't to

Americans, both past and present, and to see what the consequences of those priorities are.

The zombie apocalypse, then, is a doomsday scenario and a mode to interpret and make meaning in our shared world. It haunts me too, because those visions of the end throw annihilation and violence in our faces with startling glee rather than trepidation. The future awash in blood, gore, decay, and death. Zombies become the monsters that bring about the end of the world as we know it. They bring chaos and death. Fledgling human societies can rise from the ashes of our former worlds, but their survival is a toss-up. Zombies hang around as constant threats and reminders of what can happen to us. They show us what awaits us, and it isn't pretty.

This belief in, and desire for, the zombie apocalypse shows us again how pervasive end-times visions remain in American civic life. People still hope for them to come true. And some yearn for zombies, in particular, to manifest beyond the fictional into the realm of the real. They want zombies to show up at their doorstep because it means the world as we know it is done. The future arrives, and it's a horror story. Monsters overrun us and dismantle our lives. Some people can't wait for the end and what it might bring.

Zombies become the conduit for damage and transformation, collective and personal. Some want these monsters to tear down our present society, so we can begin anew. Some just want to kill zombies. These post-apocalyptic societies, however, are seldom better than what we have now. They are brutal and harsh, based on the idea of survival of the fittest turned up to 11. I can't imagine living in a world like this, but I don't have to because others have imagined it for public consumption. And to them, it might even look fun.

The desire for this particular apocalypse manifests in every *when* rather than *if*. *When* it comes, we will be ready. *When* it occurs, desires become actuality. We no longer imagine killing zombies, but we can actually do it. That lack of a better future society places zombie apocalypses firmly in the realm of secular apocalypticism. The world never gets better; it only gets worse. (And why would someone yearn for destruction and being left behind in a ruined world?) We are powerless to stop it, so we might as well gear up for the inevitable. It's the ruined future that some Americans look forward to because it is, at least, not what we have now.

The world is doomed—we are doomed—but at least zombies are cool.

And remember: This end comes by the hand of monsters, not through divine judgment or environmental collapse. And their monstrosity matters. Monsters, like apocalypses, *reveal*, or unveil, something about us right now. They offer truths that are hard to face. They force us to reckon with that which we would rather avoid. This is because, as cultural theorist Edward Ingebretsen points out, monsters are "showings, and tellings" that make us feel both fear and wonder.[23] We're repulsed and fascinated. We cover our eyes with our hands, but peek through our fingers.

They also serve as warnings. Monsters appear, Ingebretsen notes, to "redefine boundaries that become frayed." These are social boundaries that are starting to come apart at the seams; the ties that bind us become loosened, at best, and, at worst, cease to exist. The presence of monsters signals a social decline and the likelihood of forthcoming peril. Monsters shout, "Look, danger over here! Pay attention. Pay. Attention." But they can't make us; all they can do is warn. The rest is up to us.

Crucially, monsters are more than warnings. They appear when something has gone awry and become the way that "a community reinterprets itself."[24] When monsters appear, communities are in an identity crisis, so they have to figure out who they are and who they are not. Boundaries get reset. Limits to who can be a part of a community and who cannot get settled. The human is separated from the monster, even if the separation lacks the distance to soothe us or help us sleep at night. Monsters shore up the status quo by showing and telling what we fear and what we value.

They can bring to light what we would prefer stays in the dark.

We make monsters, and they hope we learn from them. And then, we stake them. We kill them to say who we are and what we stand for.

Americans create and consume monsters and their apocalypses, and we learn something about our culture, something far from comfortable, by paying careful attention to both. Zombie apocalypses reflect the fears and concerns of twenty-first century America. Terrorism, epidemics, social collapse, political strife, and the culture wars all appear in evocations of zombies.

Zombies represent all the things that could damn near end us. Of course, they are terrifying because of what they can reveal. And yet, some Americans want to conjure zombies and make them real. They see zombies as a literal threat to humanity, even as they eagerly wait for them to materialize. But there's more to zombies than terror. There's more to apocalypses than fear and dread. We learn much about a culture by analyzing their monsters, and zombies are America's monsters. Zombie apocalypses can't help but warn, reveal, and tell.

Zombies destroy us again and again. They end the world. And we want them to. Don't we?

It seems that we do. But why? This want, this yearning for the end, makes zombies and their apocalypses become less fantasy and more certainty. Our beliefs and actions start to make zombies seem real, and their reality has consequences. I can't help but be nervous about what this might mean about America right now. Maybe you should be, too. Maybe we all should be.

After all, the zombie apocalypse is upon us, whether we like it or not. It begins with a moan and a shamble. It likely lacks a show-stopping end and leaves us with only a whimper.

The zombies are here, and they tell a story about Americans, a story about us, that's not pretty. Their story is a warning about our human capacity for violence, fear, destruction, and hate. It tells us who we often are but also suggests that is not who we have to be.

3

"IT'S GOING TO BE A FEDERAL INCIDENT."

The CDC and the DHS Prepare for Zombies

Rule #6: Don't Be A Hero
—*Zombieland*

In May of 2011, the Centers for Disease Control and Prevention (CDC) launched a campaign for emergency preparedness that was a bit different from previous campaigns. Okay, so maybe this campaign was a lot different. It relied upon an unusual theme to convince Americans to prepare for any number of possible disasters.[1] Rather than emphasizing the typical, likely threats that we face each year, including hurricanes, earthquakes, or infectious diseases, the CDC turned their focus to zombies. That's right, the organization decided monsters would be a useful way to prepare the public for any disaster headed our way.

While the focus on zombies might seem unusual,

the CDC merely took advantage of the perpetual zombie boom and the popularity of *The Walking Dead* TV show to make preparedness more enticing. Dave Daigle, the Associate Director for Communication in the CDC's Office on Public Health Preparedness and Response, came up with the idea to use zombies. "Preparedness and public health," he told *The Atlantic*, "are not the sexiest topics."[2] Zombies, I guess, were sexy or at least sexy enough to garner attention. A fictional apocalypse might convince Americans to actually prepare for what disasters could happen and be ready if they did.

As a part of the campaign that also included Facebook posts and tweets, Dr. Ali Khan, now a retired Assistant Surgeon General and former head of the CDC's Office of Public Health Preparedness and Response, wrote a blog post called "Preparedness 101: Zombie Apocalypse." He explained how preparing for a potential—although entirely unlikely—zombie apocalypse could get Americans ready and able to handle other types of emergencies. He wrote:

> There are all kinds of emergencies out there that we can prepare for. Take a zombie apocalypse for example. That's right. I said z-o-m-b-i-e a-p-o-c-a-l-y-p-s-e. You may laugh now, but when it happens you'll be happy you read this, and hey,

maybe you'll even learn a thing or two about how to prepare for a *real* emergency.

While the threat of zombies appears laughable, silly, or far-fetched, Khan's post was a strategic move, on behalf of the CDC, to exploit zombies to do something important: pass along essential information on how to prepare for many types of disaster. This particular campaign was launched before hurricane season began on June 1st and urged those who lived in areas vulnerable to hurricanes, like me, to begin our prep for another year of potentially deadly storms.

Khan made it clear that zombies are not actually a real emergency but that their popularity gave "credence to the idea that a zombie apocalypse could happen." Some folks already wondered how they might actually prepare for that particular cataclysm, figuring out the needed supplies and weapons and deciding who they would want on their team. If zombies invaded "city streets eating anything living that got in their way," Khan pointed out, you'd probably want to know what to do ahead of time. So, he offered tips for surviving the zombie apocalypse. Planning for the zombies, it seemed, would prepare us for actual emergencies.

The CDC's guide began with the importance of having an emergency kit in your home. In case of the onslaught of the undead, Khan noted that the kit should have supplies to help you make it through your first few days post-apocalypse until you can make it to "a zombie-free refugee camp." (That escalated rather quickly.) The kit should include one gallon of water a day for each person in your home; non-perishable food; any prescription or over-the-counter medicine you might need; tools and supplies ranging from a battery-powered radio to duct tape; clothes for each person as well as bedding; and, of course, important documents like one's driver's license.

A first aid kit was also on the list, though Khan reminds us, "[Y]ou're a goner if a zombie bites you." (As if you wouldn't already know that from watching *The Walking Dead*.) First aid only goes so far when the dead rise from their graves, but with other emergencies, it would still be crucial. The list of supplies would last for around two days for the average person.

Supplies, however, wouldn't be all that you need. You'll also need a plan. Khan recommended that families develop emergency plans that include "where you would go and who you would call if zombies started appearing outside your doorstep."[3] The plan has four components: identifying what kinds of emergencies happen where you live; picking a meeting place to regroup both directly outside of your home and another beyond your neighborhood or town in case of evacuation; figuring out your emergency contacts; and planning your route for evacuations. He wrote, "When zombies are hungry, they won't stop until they get food (i.e. brains), which means you need to get out of town fast!"

Readers should be assured to know if zombies do appear, the CDC would start investigating immediately like they would in any other infectious disease outbreak. Scientists would try to figure out what caused the dead to rise and start working on a cure as quickly as possible, and federal agencies would mobilize and send out their medical teams to help first responders in zombie-infested areas.

Not only would you be ready for the zombie apocalypse by following the CDC's suggestions for preparing, but the CDC would also be ready to tackle the crisis. The government, according to this organization, could back us up against the shambling horde, but the question remains if they actually *would*. (The Trump administration's slow response to the Covid-19 pandemic does not bode well for us.) And yet, Khan suggested that the CDC would have this fictional disaster, and other more probable disasters, under control. There would be no need to panic or worry, except for the fact that there would be zombies.

Khan did show the merits of being prepared for zombies. Preparation for one calamity could help in the face of another. His advice, then, proved broadly applicable and easy to replicate. Encouraging people to be prepared is important, and it can help save lives. To be ready, you just needed to get supplies, make a plan, and stick to the plan. How hard could that be? The CDC told you what you needed and what to do, so just follow their instructions and you can make it through whatever disaster life throws at us. Preparation somehow suggests that survival can be guaranteed, even if it can't really be.

The undead become a prop to make emergency preparedness seem more fun and sexier, than it might seem normally. Why would you prepare for a more commonplace disaster, like a hurricane, when you could prepare for fictional zombies cropping up in your neighborhood? A zombie plan is more exciting than a hurricane plan. The horrors of real-life catastrophe avoided in lieu of the playfulness of gearing up for monsters. Taking on zombies also seems more manageable than confronting a Category 5 hurricane and its aftermath.

In a strange coincidence, the CDC tweeted their zombie campaign a mere five days before Christian minister Harold Camping's date for the end of the world, May 21, 2011.

In 2010 and 2011, Camping's California ministry, Family Radio, sponsored 1200 billboards to warn Americans that Judgment Day was upon us.[4] I drove by more than one of the large billboards that proclaimed,

"Cry mightily onto God (Jonah 3:8)" and "Judgment Day. May 21, 2011." A golden stamp on them further insisted, "The Bible guarantees it." Family Radio wanted us all to lament to God because the world was ending soon. The billboards were a part of a $100 million campaign to announce the date and the precise time (six p.m. in all time zones) of the Rapture, the ascension of the righteous to heaven.[5] If you weren't righteous in the way that Family Radio hoped you would be, you would be left behind on Earth to face the apocalypse and divine judgment. His faithful gave their money and time to convince others to ready themselves for what was coming and to, perhaps, get right with God.

And yet, for some, the CDC's timing seemed to be more than a case of coincidence, and both campaign and prophecy pointed to a similar thing: an apocalypse on the horizon. An apocalypse caused not by zombies but divine intervention, appearing almost simultaneously.

The end seemed to be inching a bit closer than before. The CDC's campaign, of course, was tongue in cheek; Camping and Family Radio were serious. One was humor while the other was prophecy. After all, Khan and the CDC weren't suggesting the zombie apocalypse was a real emergency—yet. Relying on the zombie apocalypse was simply a clever way to promote disaster preparedness, not to prophesize the end of our world. It was intended to convince Americans to prepare for other disasters, not fictional ones.

But intentions don't guarantee what will happen, and the reaction to Khan's advice was a bit surprising. When the zombie campaign went live, the traffic on the CDC blog jumped from the average 1000-3000 hits a day to an all-time high of 10,000 hits, and to 60,000 hits by the end of the day. Their servers promptly crashed under the weight of this web traffic.[6] They were not prepared for the response even though they had counted on the popularity of zombies to grab attention. Their servers were not entirely outfitted to handle the ambush of zombie fans. Fans eagerly read and passed along the post on social media. There was also the larger cultural interest in these monsters. Zombies were everywhere, so preparing for a zombie apocalypse was appealing and fun.

The CDC's servers did recover, and now they have a whole page dedicated to zombie social media, even featuring a graphic novella about the zombie pandemic.[7] They also posted on how *The Walking Dead* demonstrated the need for preparedness based on events from the first and second seasons of the show. (Clean water, for instance, is crucial, so keep zombies out of your water supply.) There are also zombie preparedness exercises geared toward educators, which give students the chance to experience the emergency response process by figuring out how to respond to a fictional scenario.

Zombies also brought attention to the CDC campaign in ways that they might not have predicted. Hundreds of pages of comments now accompany the initial post with wide-ranging suggestions, snark, and occasional outright derision. Many zombie fans commented on the usefulness of zombies as a way to approach emergency preparedness, while detractors complained about taxpayer dollars being wasted on silly fantasies. Some commenters suggested adding weapons and ammunition to one's emergency kit while others noted that thinking about the possibility of a zombie apocalypse led them to prepping and survivalism.

Even further for others, it seemed as if the CDC was suggesting the inevitability of zombies, and the guide became the proof of this likelihood, in spite of the CDC's claims that zombies were fantasy. If the CDC discussed these monsters, then surely zombies had to be a plausible threat. The zombie campaign made it appear that a zombie apocalypse could happen, whether they intended to or not. It wasn't an *if* as much as a *when*.

The CDC wasn't the only government agency to adopt zombies as a meme for preparation and disaster awareness. In September 2012, the Department of Homeland Security (DHS) drew on the notion of a zombie apocalypse for a public health campaign, emphasizing that "the zombies are coming." In conjunction with the DHS, the Federal Emergency Management Agency (FEMA) provided an online seminar for emergency planners nationwide.[8] Some of the DHS's rules even mimicked the famed "rules for survival" from *Zombieland* (2009). While rule 1 (cardio) and rule 4 (wear seat belts) seem applicable, the others are less so as they are more geared to harming zombies. Rules 2 (the double tap) and 25 (shoot first) make me nervous because I would hope they would only apply to zombies and not people.

Additionally, the DHS provided one thousand dollar grants for first responders and law enforcement officers to attend the HALO-Counterterrorism Summit held in San Diego, California in October 2012. This week-long training seminar covered topics like emergency preparedness, disaster response, and counterterrorism. The key event for the summit was the "Zombie Apocalypse" demonstration, a dramatic simulation of a military tactical unit facing forty zombies that was held on Halloween. (Yes, this is a bit too on the nose.) This event focused on rescuing a VIP from a village overrun with zombies while also handling team members who had been infected.

Brad Barker, the president of HALO Corp, told *The Huffington Post*, "This is a very real exercise, this is not some type of big costume party.... [T]he training is very real, it just happens to be the bad guys that we are having a little fun with." Killing zombies was more fun, it seems, than training for actual targets. And yet, Barker compared terrorists to zombies, insisting that like the monsters, terrorists were also unpredictable. Terrorists and zombies appeared easily interchangeable. The demonstration was a way to show the need for quality training and preparation in the face of volatile threats, real or fictional.[9] Preparing for one type of threat supposedly prepared you for another.

Unsurprisingly, the HALO Corp's use of zombies garnered press attention, and Barker noted that he received calls from "every whack job in the world" about whether the U.S. government was actually preparing for zombies. While Barker scoffed at the "whack job[s]," his own statements seem more ambiguous about whether zombies might be an actual threat to humanity. He said, "No doubt when a zombie apocalypse occurs, it's going to be a federal incident, so we're making it happen." Barker's use of *when* suggested the inevitability of the end of the world caused by zombies. The monsters appeared as a likely hazard that law enforcement, first responders, and soldiers could encounter. Although he ridiculed folks who imagined that the government was preparing for a zombie apocalypse, he still emphasized the usefulness of this exercise for a future scenario, and not a fictional one. His talking points made this form of doomsday seem possible or maybe even probable. The security firm's efforts, like the DHS or the CDC, appeared as proof of the threat of these monsters. The HALO Corp training, particularly the DHS grants, caught the attention of former Senator Tom Coburn, a Republican from Oklahoma. He did not approve of this use of government funds. In 2012, Coburn stated:

> [P]aying for first responders to attend a HALO Counterterrorism Summit at a California island spa resort featuring a simulated zombie apocalypse does little to discourage potential terrorists. I hope this report encourages DHS to award funds based on calculated risk, not politics.[10]

The senator's disdain for wasted taxpayer dollars revolved around the zombie simulation, which he didn't see as a useful training exercise for counterterrorism. For Coburn, terrorists, not zombies, were a real menace that required preparation and training. Watching a military tactical unit annihilate zombified actors might be good entertainment for attendees, but Coburn questioned the practicality of such a demonstration for law enforcement, first responders, soldiers, and firefighters. How likely were attendees to encounter stumbling corpses? What would they gain from participating? What kinds of skills could transfer from killing zombies to stopping terrorism?

Halo Corp, unsurprisingly, responded by pointing out that the simulation was just one component of their week-long training that included other seminars and features. Moreover, the security firm insisted that no taxpayer or DHS funds went to the "Zombie Apocalypse" event. For Coburn and other critics, the simulation appeared, at best, to be a gimmick, a fictional peril that ignored the real threats that Americans might face in an age of global and domestic terror. The specter of terrorism outweighed the entertaining fantasy of zombies, and Coburn insisted that grants like these were clear examples of the waste of government funds.

Halo Corp's "Zombie Apocalypse" and Coburn's critique demonstrate the ways in which these fictional monsters become implicated in larger discussions of terrorism, security, and safety. For Halo Corp, zombies functioned as stand-ins for terrorists because of the volatility and unpredictability of terrorism. These monsters mimicked real life threats. And yet, I remain troubled by the easy conflation of zombies and terrorists, especially considering how people of color and people from certain countries are more apt to be labeled "terrorists." White supremacists and white far-right extremists who terrorize, often are able to avoid the label altogether.

Mary McCord, a law professor at Georgetown University and a former senior Justice Department official, noted, "In the U.S., more people are killed by far-right extremists than by those who are adherents to Islamist extremism."[11] And in 2019, the Department of Homeland Security finally admitted that white supremacist terrorism is a primary security threat for the U.S.[12] and that white supremacist groups are responsible for most incidents of domestic terror. When Halo Corp imagined terrorists, I doubt they were imagining white supremacists as primary threats. Instead, terrorists emerged as zombies, dehumanized enemies that threaten our safety. Zombies were enemies, and terrorists were enemies, too. Both became less than human, monstrous even. The simulation allowed attendees to watch the military tactical unit annihilate the undead without guilt, angst, or unease. Eliminating terrorists was the goal, not intervention or prevention. Threats must be not just neutralized but obliterated, it seems, whether they were human or zombie.

Coburn, however, didn't seem to be swayed by the association of terrorists with zombies. The sheer unreality of zombies was a sticking point. Zombies were simply not possible, but terrorism always was. So, why would a counterterrorism summit employ monsters?

Learning to eliminate threats was still important, but for Coburn the threats had to be real and human.

But still, zombies emerged as the perfect foil for the CDC, the DHS, and Halo Corp for catastrophes caused by nature or humans. A zombie, after all, is a walking disaster. The monster's current popularity brought attention to the campaigns and the training because they all fit the common narratives about zombies that many of us know. They rise. Society falls. We fight back and kill them. Zombies appear as good fun, and their deaths are expected and guilt-free.

Hollywood has taught us how to react to them, and the CDC, the DHS and Halo Corp could employ the lessons we've learned by watching zombie films and TV shows. Lesson #1: Zombies are dangerous, so we must prepare for and guard ourselves against them. Lesson #2: We must be ready to destroy them. Lesson #3: Taking out zombies, even though it's dangerous, can be fun, enjoyable even. Zombies aren't human, after all. Stories about them do cultural work, often in unexpected ways.

Relying on zombies can help us prepare for a disaster or make terrorists appear as not human. Zombies, and the stories we tell about them, are never value-free. These monsters become shorthand to tell certain types of stories about the dangers of terrorism and extremists to particular audiences of military personnel, government agencies, and the general public. Zombies do stand-in for terrorists but in these trainings, humans become not just faceless enemies but monsters. They become less than human.

When we dehumanize our enemies, we can justify our violence against them as necessary and expected. Training to fight monsters means law enforcement and military personnel can come to understand any human who appears threatening as a monster who must be destroyed. The consequences of this type of training is, then, not the waste of taxpayer dollars but the lives of people who we've made into monsters. And remember, a monster is created to be staked. Humans made into monsters end up dead. These trainings are more dangerous than they originally seem. Our empathy and humanity forfeited in these zombie simulations and in everyday life.

4
"NO JOKE, THE ZOMBIE APOCALYPSE IS COMING!"
The Summer of the Walking Dead

Words have power.

—Mira Grant, *Blackout*[1]

In summer of 2012, the internet exploded with rumors about whether the zombie apocalypse had arrived. (No, I'm not kidding. This actually happened.) News story after news story appeared in mainstream media pondering whether zombies had finally appeared among us. Why? There were a series of gruesome cannibalistic crimes, so it appeared—at least to some journalists—that zombies were no longer just limited to the safe confines of fiction or film. Monsters had spilled over into the real world. The Associated Press proclaimed in a headline, "Horror movie genre becomes twisted, real-life news headline." *The Huffington Post* exclaimed, "No Joke, the Zombie Apocalypse Is

Coming!" At the heart of this speculation was the press-dubbed "Miami Zombie," a Black man who mauled and destroyed the face of a homeless white man in Miami, Florida.

The details of the case are both strange and tragic. On Saturday, May 26, 2012, thirty-one-year-old Rudy Eugene abandoned his car in South Beach and walked three and half miles along the MacArthur Causeway. While he walked, he stripped off his clothes. He then attacked sixty-five-year-old Ronald Poppo on the sidewalk of the causeway. The victim later recounted to the Miami Police Department (MPD) that Eugene's attack was unprovoked. Poppo insisted that Eugene seemed disturbed and screamed at him. Eugene smashed Poppo's face into the sidewalk, strangled him, plucked out his eyes, and chewed on his face.[2] Poppo told MPD that Eugene claimed that Poppo had stolen his Bible, which was supposed justification for the "face-eating" attack.

The MPD found scraps of Eugene's Bible at the crime scene, though Poppo claimed he had not taken it. When officers confronted Eugene, he would not stop brutalizing the face of his victim and even growled at the officers. They shot Eugene four times and killed him. At the end of the attack, more than seventy-five percent of Poppo's face was missing, and he was blind.

The motivations for the attack prove elusive, since

Eugene was shot to death shortly after the crime. We can't know why he attacked Poppo or whether his Bible was stolen or not. But this did not stop the lurid media speculation about the crime—rather the missing information seemed to generate more speculation and conspiracy theories about Eugene's motivations. Video of the attack, dubbed the "Causeway Cannibal Attack," made the rounds on the internet, and the brutal trauma Poppo survived became an easily obtained spectacle that national audiences could watch again and again. A horror movie seemed to have come to life. Poppo's pain and terror were caught on film, and empathy dissipated with every replay of the clip.

Nationwide, news reports detailed the horrible incident of cannibalism with accusations that Eugene was addled by the designer drug "bath salts," which are hallucinogenic drugs that cause rage, disorientation, and violence. The attack paired with "face eating" led the press to label Eugene the "Miami Zombie." And yet, the autopsy found no human flesh in Eugene's stomach, though the coroner noted Eugene had flesh wedged in his teeth. There was also no indication that bath salts were in his system, though the coroner did find pills in his stomach.

The Examiner claimed that Eugene's girlfriend categorized him as a pot smoker who carried his Bible with him everywhere. She later suggested that Eugene was possibly under a "voodoo curse."[3] The mention of voodoo added to the portrayal of this crime as a zombie attack. There's a longstanding connection of zombies and voodoo in American popular culture. The earliest zombie films, including *White Zombie* (1932), portrayed zombies as soulless humans under the control of a voodoo witch doctor. These images of voodoo, of course, are long-lasting stereotypes of Vodou that American filmmakers presented to audiences, far removed from actual practice. When the girlfriend supposedly pointed to a curse as a reason for his inexplicable actions, zombification appeared more plausible. The whisper of voodoo, then, seemed to add authority to the many news accounts that Eugene seemed like a zombie. Articles and newscasts transformed him into one. Add in a possible curse with the harrowing assault, and the Causeway Cannibal Attack appeared even more sensational and tantalizing to cover.

Eugene's mother, however, refused to participate in the zombie narratives about her son. She insisted that her son was not the type to be involved in such brutality. Instead, she claimed that someone must have drugged and dumped Eugene at the scene of the crime. She further noted that he must have felt threatened by Poppo in his disoriented state.[4] His mother, who did not want her name released, emphasized that Eugene was a "good kid" who regularly attended church with his two younger brothers. She told CBS News, "Everyone says he was a zombie. He was no zombie. That was my son." While news accounts dehumanized her son, Eugene's mother kept reminding interviewers that he was a person and not a monster.

His girlfriend, who also preferred to remain anonymous, also struggled with the violent portrayal of her boyfriend versus the sweet, non-violent man she loved. She emphasized, "That wasn't him, that was his body but it wasn't his spirit. Somebody did this to him." A former high school friend further noted, "Someone in their right mind doesn't do that. This is not the act of a normal person. It has to be someone under the influence."[5]

The refrain is a common one: Normal people do not act like *this*.

Something must have happened, or someone must have forced Eugene to attack. How could an otherwise non-violent person commit an act of cannibalism? How could a supposedly normal person resort to cannibalism anyway? Why would one person harm another with such extreme violence? How can we make sense of the horror of this crime? Eugene's mother, girlfriend, and friend couldn't. So, we can't explain why he attacked Poppo. Maybe this crime doesn't make sense. Maybe it never will because it is senseless. And yet, fitting the crime into certain narratives of horror helped make it make sense. Eugene's actions and Poppo's trauma became a horror story about a zombie and victim. The attack became easier to understand, if not to bear.

Nonetheless, the "Miami Zombie" generated story after story as journalists dwelled upon the explicit details of the attack. What might first appear as a rare violent act took a more sinister turn as other attacks soon surfaced: a man chopped up his roommate and consumed his heart and brain; another man ate his dog; and one man ate the lips off of a kitten. A man in New Jersey stabbed himself fifty times and threw parts of his intestines at the police, who had trouble subduing him. A mother in Texas killed her newborn, then ate part of his brain and bit off three of his toes. In St. Augustine, FL, a family discovered a naked man on their roof, who later bit the homeowner. The officers had trouble restraining him because of his unusual strength.

When a female fan bit actor Danny Bonaduce of Partridge family fame, *The Examiner* pondered if he was merely the latest victim of the zombie apocalypse. After detailing the sharp teeth of his assailant, Bonaduce blamed bath salts for the fan's biting, much like the initial claims that bath salts were responsible for Eugene's violence.[6] Bath salts were not to blame in either attack, but the idea persisted even as experts discounted it.

While one cannibalistic crime could be dismissed as a

random act of brutality, several other attacks seemed to suggest that we were on the brink of disaster. Humans were imitating zombies, or so some journalists claimed. The zombie apocalypse was upon us, or at least, the media strongly suggested that it might be. *The Examiner* queried, "Was George A. Romero right all along?"[7] Were Romero's films a warning for forthcoming doom? Was the end occurring before our eyes? These cannibalistic attacks must have been related, right?

And it wasn't just small news outlets trying to find the zombie apocalypse in other people's tragedies. Well-known, national publications were as well. *Newsweek* and the *Daily Beast* prepared a Google Map plotting all these attacks to suggest that zombies were now among us.[8] The map, still available online, demonstrates the relatively small number of these attacks rather than suggesting an overwhelming threat. It is a sad attempt at a map. If these were zombies, they were few in number, not an overwhelming epidemic. And since I'm writing now, eight years later, these attacks were clearly not the beginning of the end.

And yet to be fair to these journalists claiming the zombie apocalypse was almost here, all of these attacks did involve components of zombie lore: violent attacks, bizarre behavior, inhuman strength, and most importantly, the consumption of human flesh and organs, particularly brains. But while these tragic events seemed somewhat like the walking dead in popular culture, the connections were rather loose and not compelling. None of the perpetrators were shambling corpses. The dead hadn't risen from their graves.

Instead, they were living and breathing human beings who acted horrifically by butchering and/or murdering strangers, roommates, loved ones, and pets. Humans brutalized other humans. They were not zombies; they were not monsters. Instead, they showed how capable human beings are destroying one another. While much of the media attention to these supposed "zombie" attacks revolved around their sheer cruelty, cruelty isn't an indicator of zombies, who can't help but consume human flesh; rather, it's an indicator of humans who chose to attack people and animals.

Journalist Tony Dokoupil at the *Daily Beast* asked, "What's with all the craziness?" as if craziness was a useful description of what was happening rather than a way to pathologize people. He further quipped, "Memorial Day feel[s] like end times."[9] What he wanted to know was what might lead people to act in such violent, socially taboo ways? Dokoupil wondered if maybe the internet was blurring the boundaries between reality and fantasy. Maybe each attacker couldn't tell what was real anymore. Maybe the rest of us couldn't either. The internet age might prove more dangerous to us than we could have imagined. Or perhaps, he was looking for something easy to blame for this societal collapse, and the internet fit the bill.

His article, however, conveniently ignored the ways in which media coverage also blurred the supposedly demarcated lines between real life and imagination. With every headline that speculated about or declared the possibility of the zombie apocalypse, the media became complicit in the fervor. Yet the boundaries between the real and the fictional are ever so porous. We want them to be firm, solid, and impenetrable, but instead, things slide through. Fantasy sometimes pops up where we least expect it, and reality sometimes appears fictional. Art imitates life, but remember the inverse is true too: life so often imitates art. So, I remain unsurprised that zombies appear when and where we might not expect them to be in random attacks or preparedness campaigns. Fantasy can stalk our waking hours, too.

The Examiner went further than the *Daily Beast* by having "experts," primarily novelists who write about zombies, weigh in on the possibility of an "invasion of the living dead." Jonathan Mayberry, author of the Joe Ledger series, explained that these attacks were likely not the beginning of the end at the hands of zombies, but rather "it is becoming easier to believe that some kind of devastating pandemic is poised to hit." Mira Grant (pseudonym for Seanan McGuire), author of the Newsflesh trilogy, emphasized the tragedy of these gruesome crimes that demonstrate "how unrealistic reality can get."[10] Reality sometimes appeared more akin to horror films than we might like.

"I think the world is going to the zombies soon," noted Zomboid, a commenter at *UWeekly*, a college newspaper.[11] Like other commenters, Zomboid was convinced that these "zombie" attacks signaled a forthcoming apocalypse. In these cannibalistic attacks, zombies appeared real, authentic even, and for some, this provided evidence that the end of the world from shuffling hordes was no longer just a fictional endeavor. George Romero seemed prescient or prophetic. The end would appear not with a bang or a whimper, but with cannibalism, brutality, and maybe even some shambling.

Due to mounting online speculation about zombies in the summer of 2012, the CDC even felt pressure to comment. Even though the CDC employed zombies as a method to make disaster preparedness fun, the supposed zombie attacks prompted the agency to declare that these monsters were fictional. The CDC's spokesperson David Daigle explained to *The Huffington Post* that the "CDC does not know of a virus or condition that would reanimate the dead." Monsters, the CDC tried to remind us, are make-believe. *The Huffington Post*, however, was not yet ready to relinquish the possibility of zombies. They reported "zombie-like characteristics" apparent among ants, which had consumed a recently discovered fungus in the Brazilian rainforest.[12] The fungus dominated the ant's brain and moved its body around. Eventually, the fungus killed its host. Surely zombified ants demonstrated that something similar could happen to humans. Science rather than science fiction informed the article. If ants could become zombies, then maybe it wasn't a stretch to think humans could too.

Whether zombie ants or the "Miami Zombie," these examples seemed to suggest—to some people—that a zombie apocalypse was probable, even if the world did not end in summer of 2012. (And it didn't, and it still hasn't yet.)

Rudy Eugene's actions appeared as an anomaly that captivated audiences for a short span of time. The media coverage drew upon the popularity of zombies to explain the violence of his attack on Ronald Poppo, who now resides at a nursing home due to the severity of his injuries. The prevalence of the zombie apocalypse in film, on television, and in fiction meant that this narrative was hastily applied to Eugene. It proved as convenient as it was attention-grabbing. While he might have appeared like a zombie, the media coverage attempted to make this a bigger story about the beginning of the end. And in the process, the media made Eugene into something less than human, a monster, to generate clicks on their sites. His life mattered less than the wild speculation about zombies.

His legacy was no longer his own. Instead, Eugene became a terrifying spectacle meant to frighten and entertain viewing audiences and readers. The media made him into a monster, and once he was a monster, he no longer required our empathy or compassion. This event was a tragedy for Poppo and Eugene, and it deserved to be treated like one rather than jokingly emerging as the beginning of an apocalypse that never arrived.

5

"ARE YOU ABLE TO SHOOT YOUR KID IN THE FACE?"

Doomsday Preppers and the Zombie Apocalypse

You will be torn apart by teeth or bullets.
—Morgan, *The Walking Dead*

In April of 2013, the officers at Fort Sam Houston, Texas, relied on zombies as a way to get soldiers ready for hurricane preparedness. They put on the U.S. Army-North's Hurricane Rehearsal of Concept drill. The keynote speaker for the event was Max Brooks, who discussed the importance of preparation for survival.

If you don't already know, Max Brooks is one of the authors most associated with the genre of books about the zombie apocalypse. His popular *Zombie Survival Guide* (2003) is a clever and funny take on survival guides, which usually offer up advice on how to advance your career, learn a language, play an instrument, or make it in the wilderness. His book, instead, is about how to outlast the impending onslaught of the undead. He also wrote *World War Z* (2007). It's a novel, written in the style of an oral history, about a global war against zombies and the end of human civilization as we know it now.

Like other how-to products, the *Zombie Survival Guide* instructs the reader on what exactly to do if these monsters suddenly appear. The book covers the origins of zombies, the likelihood of the zombie apocalypse, and helpful tips for weathering this type of apocalypse. Brooks includes handy comparisons of the weapons that you might use to make it through. No matter what weapon you choose, remember to aim for the brains. He offers up advice about appropriate clothing and transportation. A wet suit, for instance, might seem like good protection from zombie bites, but it really isn't. He even explains what materials you'll need to make your home zombie-proof. Planning and preparing for the inevitable zombie plague is as easy as purchasing, reviewing, and following the guide. The more resources you have at your disposal, the readier you will be.

Brooks, then, was an obvious choice for a keynote at the disaster-preparedness drill, but there's more going on here than the author simply being a zombie expert. Reporter Spencer Ackerman noted that Brooks is "a cult hero inside the Army" and continued, "I've found his books on practically every forward operating base I've been on in Iraq and Afghanistan." His books appealed to soldiers, according to Ackerman, not because of the references to the military but because the "heroes" of his books are not people—the humans who fight monsters—but the *practices* that they use to survive. How you prepare—what you do—matters much more than who you are. Preparation is the most essential thing you can do, if you want to survive in an undead world.

Even though the *Guide* is, well, about zombies, it *feels* applicable to so many other possible disasters, like hurricanes, which require significant planning, prep, and recovery efforts. When the worst happens, if you've read Brooks' books, you might be ready if you listened to his warnings and took the time to prepare yourself for what comes next. It's no surprise that his books, with their messages about the importance of preparation, appealed to soldiers.

So, back to the Army's mock hurricane drill. Zombies were, once again, a stand-in for a natural disaster, a case study to think about the logistics of disaster planning and the actions required to prepare and manage a crisis. Hurricane preparedness, after all, requires plans for mass evacuations, for rescue and retrieval, and administration of recovery efforts. This task, according to Ackerman, is "[n]ot exactly *unlike* the task in *World War Z*, which is to reconstitute civilization while managing the zombie problem."[1] Disasters require trying to figure who and what can be saved, reckoning with all that's lost, and rebuilding in the ruins. Disasters destroy and recreate the world, even if we don't notice that they do. There are big catastrophes and smaller ones that happen every day. At least we usually don't also have to manage zombies.

For the CDC, the DHS, Halo Corp and the Army, relying upon zombies helped them plan, prepare, and oversee disasters while the popularity of the monsters piqued the interest of the public and, maybe, convinced them that they also needed to be prepared. Zombies make emergency preparedness seem fun and playful rather than terrifyingly necessary. These monsters are never a real threat, unlike hurricanes, tornados, earthquakes, flooding, pandemics, or other catastrophes. Planning for zombies becomes a low stakes way to engage potential life-threatening dangers.

Perhaps it feels less dire when we contemplate zombies at the door rather than hurricanes ripping through our homes and laying waste to our communities. Perhaps zombies seem easier to handle than the raging forest fires that decimated parts of California; the Category 5 hurricane that walloped where I now live in north Florida in 2019; or a global pandemic, Covid-19, with a staggering body count and a potential vaccine months and months away from being available. Perhaps preparing for fictional ends can prepare us for the dangers that we don't even want to consider but are far more likely. Zombies might seem like a gimmick to cajole us into planning and preparing, and they are. But these campaigns attempt to convince us, all of us, to take seriously the possibility that we will face some kind of disaster. Catastrophes are inevitable, so we should be ready.

Preparing for zombies might prepare us for anything that comes our way. Or they might not, but military personnel, CDC officials, and a security firm think they will.

It's no surprise, then, that zombies are also popular beyond government agencies. Civilian emergency preparedness groups have turned to zombies, too. One example is the now defunct Zombie Response Team (ZRT). The organization was operational in 2013, when I was first writing this book, but is no longer. Still, their example is worthwhile to consider, so I am.

Founded in 2010 by Morgan Barnhart, Josh Garcia, and Dan Parker, the organization was based in San Antonio, Texas. *San Antonio Magazine* reported that ZRT had been getting ready for the apocalypse since 2000, even if the organization didn't exist officially until ten years later.[2] Their mission statement was "to protect and sever," a cute play on the common motto of police departments "to protect and serve."

According to ZRT's former website, the organization sought to "create the biggest enterprise of individuals ready to fight the undead, as well as to help others." Like the Army's training, ZRT used zombies to promote emergency preparedness because "[i]f you can survive a zombie apocalypse, you can survive anything." Preparing for zombies, folks suggest over and over, can make us ready for any catastrophe and possibly even the end of the world.

In 2013, I interviewed co-founder Barnhart over email. She explained to me the ZRT emerged from both a common interest in zombies as well as the desire to help people learn how to prepare for and survive disasters. She noted, "We decided to combine our theories of 'what if the zombies attack, what would we do' into...real, practical guidance to be able to withstand any disaster or emergency situation."

For Barnhart, these monsters were particularly useful for training because of the longstanding relationship between fictional portrayals of zombies and disease. On screens and in books, viruses are often the reason the dead rise and crave human flesh. A disease "that spreads on a mass scale, in a short period of time" could create the living dead. These monsters become a common stand-in for the volatility of pandemics. Zombies, like diseases, are seemingly unstoppable, unpredictable, and mindless. Barnhart explained:

[T]hey just keep going and going and going until

they get double tapped or they decompose. That's pretty scary! Vampires keep their sense about them (for the most part) [and] werewolves only change on a full moon...In general, nothing else is as scary as a mindless zombie.

Zombies might be scary but preparing for them doesn't seem to be. ZRT's thousands of members globally appeared to agree. In our interview, Barnhart claimed to have ZRT members from 11 to 65 years old, many of whom were Boy Scouts as well as current and retired military personnel. She also emphasized the diversity of the organization's membership as well. (Though it's not entirely clear what she meant by diversity.)

Preparing for zombies is appealing. After all, was there a better way to educate the general public about being prepared for a more natural disaster than zombies? ZRT seemed to think not.

And education was a core component of ZRT's mission. In 2013, their website, which no longer exists, included a multitude of advice for potential and current zombie preppers. There were articles on how to prepare a "bug out bag," a bag with supplies that will last 72 hours; a list of necessary items that will help you survive the zombie apocalypse (boots, food, first aid, weapons, etc.); and even a discussion of the "right mindset" for survival (Be positive!). Additionally, ZRT weighed in on how large or small one's team should be to best improve the chances for survival. Rather than tell members which team size was more efficient, ZRT provided the pros and cons for each size group: duo (two people), small group (two to five people), and big group (five to twenty people). While a larger group might initially seem to be the best option, ZRT warned that bigger groups "can become a liability," and they would keep you from the important work of "hunting down zombies."

In addition to advice, the website also offered a forum for members to communicate and a store that sold a variety of products branded by ZRT. The store included beanies, hats, bracelets, tank tops, t-shirts, patches, flashlights, a flint kit, a mini-crossbow, a machete, a stainless steel water bottle, and several different decals. I found myself partial to the mini-crossbow, even though I remain doubtful the smaller arrows could actually take down a lurching monster. The store gave members a chance to show their dedication to ZRT by purchasing merchandise, which proudly displayed that they were a part of the team.

One item in their store, in particular, drew my attention. It was a poster of Uncle Sam as a ZRT team member wearing a hat and tactical vest with a gun strapped to his back. Uncle Sam glared as he pointed his finger at the American public. The poster declared, "WE

WANT YOU FOR Z.R.T." If Uncle Sam is even ready for doomsday, why aren't you? Patriotism and preparation for zombies appear side-by-side. I didn't realize that killing zombies would ever be considered patriotic. I'm not sure it should be.

In addition to being a cofounder of ZRT, Barnhart also wrote a book, *Could the Zombie Apocalypse Become a Reality?* (2012), which examines the potential ways that the zombie pandemic could actually occur. She pointed to variants of known diseases like rabies as a possible cause of zombification. However, she assured readers that the book was not "written to frighten" us, but rather to "inform" us about what could cause a "real life type of zombie apocalypse."[3] Diseases mutate, after all, so why couldn't common illnesses dramatically change in ways that would result in humans transforming to zombies? (I hope they can't. I need to be able to sleep at night.)

Like so many other people, Barnhart looked to nature for evidence of how zombies might already exist. Of course, the example that she pointed to was zombie ants. Everyone, it seems, loves to use these poor ants to make the point that living dead could become really real. The ants, whose brains are hijacked by a fungus, continue to do the work of convincing people that humans could become mindless monsters. It feels like a stretch to make those kinds of connections. And it's a heavy burden, the existence of zombies, to keep placing on such a tiny creature. Still, there are those who like to claim that zombies are already here, or at least zombie ants are, but maybe they don't follow Hollywood's typical portrayal.

When I asked Barnhart if she thought the zombie apocalypse was a real possibility, she commented, "Anything is possible." These monsters could appear beyond fantasy. If anything is possible, then zombies could be possible. If zombies are possible, then we need to be preparing for their arrival and the downfall of civilization. ZRT, then, encouraged folks to prepare just in case there is a zombie emergency (not just a prank involving an emergency alert) and the apocalypse is suddenly our reality.

After all, when zombies arrive, it's a little late to start stocking up on all you need to survive or to learn how to use your equipment. You must start prepping now, *right now*, if you are going to be ready for what comes next. So, ZRT wanted folks not only to join their organization (and maybe buy a t-shirt or decal) but also to train with all your tools. Using them should become "second nature." Practice can make you prepared but not necessarily perfect. Practice can maybe make you ready enough to outlast the undead.

ZRT was an organization that was a subset of the larger prepper community, those who avidly prepare or "prep" for survival in the face of any disaster. Barnhart explained to me, "As far as we're concerned, if you're a prepper, you're a part of our community and we're a part of yours; we all help each other." Any prepper could count as a zombie apocalypse prepper, I guess.

And zombie apocalypse preppers are, of course, not the only ones getting ready for the world to end. There are "doomsday preppers" who prep for various types of potential doomsdays. These folks caught national attention with the airing of National Geographic's reality show, *Doomsday Preppers*, in 2012. The show, which ran for four seasons, followed "ordinary Americans" readying for the end of the world. Preppers embrace survivalism, stockpile food, supplies, ammunition, and other items, and train for life after the apocalypse. They seek to be ready when their chosen form of disaster strikes.

The show received mixed reviews with some critics disturbed by the fatalism of preppers who posit that the world will end soon and that humans are powerless to stop it from happening. But the second season premiere proved to be National Geographic Channel's highest rated premiere in 2012 with more than one million people watching. Prepping, at least, appears to be fascinating to watch, if not to actively do.

Doomsday preppers, *National Geographic* shows us, are not a monolith, and they disagree on how the world might end: economic collapse, nuclear annihilation, natural disasters, government shutdown, or some sort of vague social demise. The show documents how different people prep while also pointing out the flaws in each of their plans. How can you really prepare for living in a nuclear wasteland? (And why would you want to? I sure don't.)

But while prepping might seem out of the ordinary, marginal even, it isn't. Richard Laycock reported on a *Finder* survey about how many Americans participate in doomsday prep, and the numbers are higher than even I imagined that they would be. The 2017 survey found that 20% of Americans purchased survival supplies in the last year. That's almost 52 million people. Another 35% of Americans admitted that they didn't have to purchase supplies in the last year because they already *had them*. That's another 89 million people. Laycock wrote, "Adding up the numbers, that's roughly 55% of American adults (141 million adults) who are prepping for the end times. Paranoid much?"[4] One hundred and forty-one million Americans have done some form of prep or honed their survival skills. Prepping isn't as much of an outlier as it might seem.

But I'm not as confident as those at *Finder* that all of these Americans are hardcore doomsday preppers. Instead, I think most of those surveyed are preparing for what they imagine is an uncertain and possibly hostile future. That's still a significant amount of Americans who've purchased supplies, survival kits, and/or weapons; put money into savings; renovated homes; acquired transportation in case of evacuation; and taken self-defense classes or survival courses.

Prepping, then, appeals to even those who don't think the apocalypse is beating down our doors and just want to be ready for whatever disaster might be awaiting us in the future. So, it shouldn't be surprising that preppers at all levels of engagement are always looking for new ways to be ready and new things to be purchased. Take for example the Self-Reliance Expo, which Tim Murphy reported on for *Mother Jones*. It was a 2012 key readiness trade show that offered everything from dehydrated food to tactical gear. He estimated the market for disaster preparedness and survivalism to be at around $500 million from stockpiles of food to weapons to bunkers. Prepping proved profitable to all of those shopping their wares at the show and online, but it is also an expensive endeavor to undertake. For *Money*, Matt Bemer reported that the CDC's basic survival kit of food, water, first aid would cost over $450 per person, so a kit for a family of four would be over $1800.[5] The CDC's recommendations, of course, didn't include fancy gear or weapons, which are pricey additions to any survival kit. To be prepared for anything requires quite a bit of money that many could not afford.

Prepping is also political, and Murphy documented the political and racial dynamics of prepping too. The

Expo occurred ten days before the 2012 presidential election, and Murphy found that preppers were worried about the possible re-election of President Barack Obama and the danger that his continued presidency supposedly posed to the nation's well-being. Preppers feared his re-election, particularly because they were afraid that the first Black president would support stricter gun control legislation or even the possible confiscation of guns.

James Talmage Stevens, also known as Doctor Prepper, told Murphy that the prepper market (serious preppers versus the more casual ones) is only about four million people, who are mostly "white upper-middle class." One of the prevalent fears of the preppers that Murphy interviewed was breakdown of the economy. They feared that an economic crisis could lead to unrest, crime, and lawlessness. All preppers want to be ready for when TSHTF, or "the shit hits the fan." [6] Disaster could be possible at any time, so readiness and defense were both essential. And disaster seemed more imminent to these preppers if Obama was to be president for four more years. Preppers, mostly white people who could easily afford to prep, were deeply worried about what Obama's re-election would mean for them and how it might impact them.

While the preppers that Murphy documents tend to prepare for social and economic collapse, some in the prepper community insistently pointed to zombies as a likely cause for the downfall of society, not just as a part of an emergency preparedness campaign. Prompted by the "face eating attack" in Miami, some preppers started collecting more supplies of both food and weapons and then posted pictures of their "stashes" online.[7] Being prepared was important, but documenting one's supplies demonstrated to the larger world who would actually survive a calamity.

On December 17, 2012, the Discovery Channel aired *Zombie Apocalypse*, a show examining the so-called "zombie preppers" who were readying themselves for the end of the world by the infected mouths of zombies. The show primarily focuses on four preppers: Matthew Oakey, a firearms specialist; Patti Heffernan, a mother of two; Shawn Beatty, a high school teacher; and Alfredo Carbajal, the founder of the Kansas Anti-Zombie Militia (KAZM). Pivoting between scientists and other experts who discuss the prospect of a zombie pandemic and the interviews with the preppers, the show gives a glimpse of those who believe in a forthcoming zombie apocalypse. Its tagline: "Zombies are real… They're just not what you think." On screen, Carbajal of the KAZM ominously noted that it is "not a question of if but when." Again, I find myself stuck on the insistence of *when*. The milder *if* must appear too wishy-washy to communicate a future end. *When* suggests plausibility; *if* remains mired in ambiguity. All of this preparation only makes sense with the certainty of *when*, otherwise all this effort and energy was wasted on an event that would never come to pass.

Unsurprisingly, the show marks May 26, 2012, as the beginning of the end, which was the day that Rudy Eugene brutally attacked Ronald Poppo in Miami. Eugene is forever remembered as a zombie, not a person, and Poppo is forever attacked, on repeat, and appears as the first victim of the zombie apocalypse that some want to happen. Of course, Discovery included footage of the attack in the show because it supposedly looks like, and maybe, just maybe, is a zombie attack. It doesn't appear so to me, but it does for all four preppers. We get to watch Eugene maul Poppo again as if watching the violence over and over will suddenly confirm the existence of zombies.

For Heffernan particularly, fiction had become reality. With additional cannibalistic crimes in the U.S. and globally, these isolated events appeared connected. Something larger in the works that only those interviewed could truly see. Zombies did not rise from graves, but instead, they already existed among us. Humans acted like zombies. Be it drugs, government experiments, or viruses, the movie monsters could emerge in real life, and Eugene's vicious assault marked the beginning of the end. Zombies might be real because humans acted monstrously.

Intriguingly, the four zombie preppers insisted that there was more to this crime than the public knew. There was a possibility of a conspiracy, and in the documentary, conspiracy theory had a starring role. More than the others, the firearms specialist Oakey feared some form of government cover-up and suggested the government was somehow responsible for the "Miami Zombie." Discovery traced the possible conspiracy theories from biomedical research gone wrong, secret government drug experiments, and even floated the idea that rogue voodoo priests were creating zombies.

Whether it be a particular conspiracy or something else, each prepper had their own reasons for prepping. Heffernan insisted that the biggest threat to her family was zombies—not car accidents, drowning, cancer, or the other more mundane ways to die. She emphasized, "Even my daughter knows we only shoot zombies in the head." When she imagined what might happen if zombies bit her husband or children, she looked pained. The vision of such a terrible fate, becoming monsters, for her children proved distressing to her. Yet in a later conversation with high school teacher Beatty, Heffernan declared, "If you've got a bite, I will shoot you in the face." While she might have agonized over ending the lives of bitten loved ones, infected strangers were another matter entirely. They had to die.

Carbajal emphasized that the zombie apocalypse "can be a reality" and provided Discovery with a tour of the KAZM's fenced compound equipped with an underground bunker. This organization stockpiled non-perishable foods, bottled water, water filtration systems, and a variety of weapons. Men wearing camouflage and bandanas displayed the guns, machetes, and grenades. When Oakey visited the militia compound, he asked members of the KAZM what they would do if loved ones were bitten, which led to a heated conversation amongst members. One man asked, "Are you able to shoot your kid in the face?" Another responded with affirmation and profanity. Some asserted that they are not your kids anymore if they become infected. Others expressed dismay at the possibility of killing their children, even if they were zombies. One particular member declared that he would shoot zombie children, even if the others can't.

The KAZM, after all, is preparing for war against zombies. Once bitten, a human is no longer a human but a monster. It becomes a battle for human survival. Battles have casualties. Humans have to step up to protect themselves, even if the threat is child zombies. Any human, including children, can become monsters, and monsters have to die for humans to survive.

Watching their disturbing conversation on my laptop

screen made me think of the first episode of AMC's *The Walking Dead*. There's a scene that's haunted me ever since I watched it in 2010. One of the show's protagonists, Sheriff Rick Grimes (Andrew Lincoln), encounters a little girl wearing a nightgown and holding a teddy bear. At first, he thinks she's lost and in need of help. As he approaches her, she begins to growl at him. When Rick gets a closer look at her, he sees her bloodstained nightgown and realizes that she is a zombie. He shoots her in the head. When I watched this scene with my partner, he turned to me and said, "This show might be rough." As any fans of the show know, he was right.

While a fictional character shooting a fictional child is disturbing, the scene we watched was only part of a television show. Listening to members of the Kansas Anti-Zombie Militia debating about whether to shoot their children was a different matter entirely. It was jarring to witness. At first, I had a hard time believing that they were serious, but their commitment to destroying zombies, even zombies who used to be their children, was serious. More than anything else from the show, this argument, this moment, bothered me. Frankly, I was a bit stunned by such a casual exchange about murdering their children. I shouldn't be, but I am. Imagining my children as zombies led me to a different conclusion. I wouldn't even consider harming them, even if they transformed into zombies. They would probably bite me because *I would let them*. This is when I realized that I would not survive a zombie apocalypse, which was something that I already expected. No amount of prep could save me from my feelings. No argument would convince me to shoot anyone in the face. I would be a goner. I'm okay with that.

In a 2012 *New York Times* review of *Zombie Apocalypse*, Neil Genzlinger noted that the zombie preppers documented are unconvincing about the possible zombie threat. What bothered Genzlinger about the show is that "it is full of people detailing their plans for blasting away zombies and discussing things like whether they would be able to shoot their own children if they were to become infected." He writes that the program is "almost unwatchable" because the Newtown school shooting occurred only days before.[8]

The discussions about possible violence against loved ones cannot be detached from the real-life horror of the deaths of six adults and twenty children, all between six and seven years of age, at Sandy Hook Elementary. At *The Los Angeles Times*, Patrick Kevin Day also made this connection: "[T]he zombie fad is having a disturbing ripple effect on public consciousness."[9] Indiscriminate violence and killing are essential parts of zombie movies, TV shows, and books. Monsters, who were once human, get killed no matter who they used to be, even if they are children. Zombie preppers' willingness to kill their own children if they become monsters shouldn't surprise us. But it should disturb us. Their ability to dehumanize others, not just strangers but their loved ones too, is too close to the reality of mass shootings and gun violence more generally. It's way too easy to destroy someone who isn't understood as human. It's also depressingly common.

Day's piece also notes the supposed zombie attacks, the CDC's denial of zombies, and the Halo Corp counterterrorism summit as examples of the virulence of this fad. Intriguingly, he proclaims, "Zombies aren't real," as if to assure his audience that zombie preppers cannot possibly believe in zombies, nor should we. A refrain attempting to claim that something that's not real can't hurt us. A way to say that we should not prepare for something that's not real or is even a possibility.

His proclamation, however, wouldn't sway zombie preppers. They are already invested in the potential of zombies to bring about doomsday. They already shifted *if* to *when*. They already know who to shoot and when to shoot them. They have already prepared for something that might not be real but definitely can hurt us. And I can't help but wonder who the biggest threat is. Is it really the monsters? Or is it the people who are getting ready for monsters with survival kits and guns?

It's not the monsters that we have to worry about, but

rather all those people who would shoot us in the face. People are more dangerous than the monsters. They could decide that any of us are monsters at any moment. When they decide that we are threats or enemies, we become disposable. Once we are considered monsters, our lives no longer matter, and that should make us all worried.

6
"WE HATE ALL ZOMBIES."
The Intimate Relationship Between Zombies and Guns

My mama always told me someday I'd be good at something. Who'd a guessed that something'd be zombie-killing?
—Tallahassee, *Zombieland*

In early December of 2012, Jared Gurman of Long Island, NY, shot his girlfriend Jessica Gelderman over an argument about the AMC's *The Walking Dead*. The argument started because Gurman asserted that the military would cause an apocalyptic event that would inevitably lead to zombies, and Gelderman disagreed and insisted that the zombie apocalypse wouldn't happen. Her refusal to even consider the possibility of the apocalypse made Gurman angry. He had already been drinking. After their argument heated up, Gelderman left their shared apartment, and Gurman started sending her threats via text message. Concerned about the texts, Gelderman eventually returned to the apartment at 2:30 a.m. to check in on her boyfriend. When she arrived, Gurman was sitting on the stairs with his .22 semi-automatic rifle. She attempted to calm him down. As she walked up the stairs, he shot her once in the back and then took her to the hospital. He later explained that his drinking made him paranoid. Gurman was arrested and charged with second degree attempted murder.[1] Later, he pled guilty to first degree assault and is serving jail time.[2]

While it might seem far-fetched that an argument about the reality of zombies could lead to actual violence, this shooting suggests otherwise. Granted, Gurman was intoxicated and admittedly paranoid, but he could not handle his girlfriend's refusal to consider that these monsters could become real. He also bought into similar conspiracies to those adopted by the zombie preppers in the previous chapter, who believed that the government might end up being responsible for an outbreak of the undead. While Gurman's insistence that zombies might be real seems like a silly or trivial conviction, it had high stake consequences for the injured Gelderman, a punctured lung and broken ribs. Imaginary monsters had the potential to incite violence.

Believing in the mere possibility of the zombie apocalypse led to attempted murder.

Gurman's attempt at murdering his girlfriend demonstrates the intimate relationship of zombies to American gun culture. In popular culture, killing zombies requires weapons, lots of them, and usually these weapons are guns. Zombie films often feel like homage to the gun with characters taking out one zombie after another. They all know how to load, shoot, and reload a gun, and their guns never seem to misfire. The characters never seem to miss their target; their shots are improbably accurate.

Take, for example, *Zombieland* (2009), a comedic twist on standard zombie movies, which follows the sole survivors of the zombie apocalypse, Columbus (Jesse Eisenberg), Tallahassee (Woody Harrelson), Wichita (Emma Stone), and Little Rock (Abigail Breslin), as they travel in what is left of the United States. Creative ways to kill zombies, the "zombie kill of the week," is a running gag in the movie. A nun kills a zombie by dropping a piano on it, and Tallahassee uses baseball bats and gardening shears to massacre the undead. But guns and violence remain fast friends throughout *Zombieland*. All of the survivors, men and women, rely on guns to survive a zombie-infested world. In one particular scene, Tallahassee fights a horde of zombies in an amusement park, Pacific Playland. He draws them to him and then hunkers down in the booth of a carnival game. Using guns and more guns, he appears to have annihilated almost all of the zombies in the park. The corpses of these monsters pile up around the booth as his vengeance for the death of his young son is realized bullet by bullet.

Guns emerge as crucial for survival against zombies in the movies and also in real life. Fans, preppers, and interested others avidly discuss which weapons will best serve you if the undead appear. Remember that Max Brooks listed the pros and cons of various weapons in *The Zombie Survival Guide*. It isn't really surprising then that gun and ammunition manufacturers as well as outdoor merchandisers create, market, and sell a variety of zombie killing tools and accessories. They found another niche market to sell to, so they do. Preparation equals survival, and purchasing is a part of preparation. These purchases bring assurance that you can make it through a zombie apocalypse unlike all those people who didn't prepare.

Hornady Manufacturing Company, a manufacturer of ammunition and handloading tools based in Nebraska, released Zombie Max ammunition in 2011. It came in nine different cartridge sizes, which cost from $21 to $39. The ammo is no longer in production but proved to be popular when it was sold. The promotional materials, previously on their website, urged, "Be PREPARED—

supply yourself for the Zombie Apocalypse." Zombie Max was specially designed to kill zombies, though Hornady warns that it was "live" ammunition, not a toy. Thus, "[n]o human being, plant, animal, vegetable, or mineral should ever be shot" with this ammunition. And yet, these were live rounds for fictional monsters.

Hornady wasn't alone in creating products associated with zombies. Gerber Gear, an Oregon-based company well-known for their knives and gear, has an Apocalypse Survival Kit. It's out of stock on Gerber Gear's website, though still available on Amazon for a little over $325. Their kit contained three machetes, three knives, an axe, and a durable carrying case and made an appearance on the second season of *The Walking Dead*. The product description, of course, points to zombies:

> What if humanity's worst fears are realized? If the dead walk, the continuation of the human race will become a daily struggle. Survival will come down to being prepared—are you? The best chance lies in Gerber's Apocalypse Kit.

Being prepared was the only way to survive, and purchasing a kit was a way to be prepared. With this kit, "[t]he undead will regret stumbling upon your doorstep."[3]

Henry Miller Outdoors noted that the zombie

apocalypse is "the new tactical." Labeling products "tactical" was a marketing trend, and zombies appeared to be the new catchy label for outdoor gear.[4] Knives, axes, and bullets were marketed as especially for killing the walking dead. What is so interesting about these products is that they are marketed as actual weapons and gear, but their intended targets are imaginary. Fans can purchase these bullets or machetes, but no zombies exist for the weapons' use. Yet. Well, preppers would say *yet*.

Intriguingly, in December of 2012, the *Huffington Post* pointed to a spike in gun sales and background checks after Black Friday, the day after Thanksgiving that is often considered the first day of Christmas shopping.[5] ABC News reported that gun stores could not keep up with the demand for guns and ammo. Gun store owners attributed this to the re-election of President Obama, the zombie obsession, and doomsday prep more generally. Steve Parsons, the owner of the Houston Armory (a gun store), told ABC that he couldn't keep Hornady's Zombie Max in stock.[6] While the reelection of President Obama and fears about gun control might seem expected (yet still troubling) as reasons for gun sales, how are we to understand the inclusion of zombies? Why were zombies on the minds of gun purchasers? When did a movie monster become a reason for purchasing weapons?

The popularity of zombie films and *The Walking Dead*

definitely contributed to the rise of zombie marketing for weapons and zombie targets, but it doesn't entirely explain this interest. In 2012, *Guns and Ammo* produced a special issue ("Zombie Nation") about this fad with a featured article on an AR-15 assault rifle modified for zombie killing. At *Salon*, Marc Herman reported on Spike's Tactical, a Florida company that created a zombie trigger assembly for the AR-15 with a selector that has three options—"live," "dead," or "undead." The zombie trigger sold so well that it has been on backorder.[7] Herman emphasized that the zombie fad in guns and ammo allows for new weapons and accessories that "dance on the edge of gun-law loopholes." While high power weapons might appear useful for killing the resurrected dead, Herman wrote, "it's harder to justify in non-zombie settings." I certainly hope this is the case, but I wonder.

Indeed, high-power and high-caliber weapons for zombie killing employ fantasy to rationalize the purchase and ownership of guns that might otherwise violate gun laws. Has the rise of zombie culture become a method to work around existing gun legislation? Do products made for killing zombies allow fantasy to trump reality? It seems so. I can't help but think about the consequences of marketing real weapons for fantasy targets. Weapons for killing zombies can also maim, harm, and kill humans. Telling someone not to use guns and ammo on anything except the undead doesn't guarantee that they actually will. It's a warning that removes liability from the company that issued it, not a rule that has to be followed. Who are the zombies that purchasers really want to eradicate? Who might these zombies represent in real life? We don't have to dig deep to find the clues.

Alongside zombie weapons, there is also a burgeoning market for zombie targets, both paper and 3D, to practice using those weapons and others like them. Paper targets come in a variety of zombie characters from clowns to brides and grooms. But simulating a zombie apocalypse becomes easier with eerily realistic 3D targets. One such producer of these targets is Zombie Industries. They offer a line of 3D bleeding zombie targets "designed to help YOU prepare for the next Zombie outbreak that our World's leaders, even to this very day, are keeping top-secret." Conspiracy still goes hand-in-hand with any mention of the zombie apocalypse. The hand-painted zombies are made in the USA and seek to "resemble an infected human that just finished gnawing your neighbor." This supposedly realistic appearance helps "you really feel the hate."

In 2013, the line of bleeding targets contained 15 different models: five animals (including a zombified pig or kangaroo), an alien, a clown, a Nazi, a terrorist (who was reminiscent of Osama bin Laden), a TV director/producer, an ex-girlfriend, a grave digger, "Chris," "Leo," and "Rocky" (who all look like ordinary dudes just zombified). The prices ranged from $49.95-$89.95. Additionally, they had a "Sons of Guns" Apocalypse kit ($15,999.95), which included 250 3D zombie targets as well as 250 ZOMBOOM! exploding rifle targets that can be placed inside the zombies to make them explode when they are shot. By 2020, the options had dwindled. There are now only seven bleeding 3D targets, including two different clowns, a terrorist (who still looks like bin Laden), "Chris," "Rocky," "Kevin," and a Nazi, and their Apocalypse kit is no longer on the website at all. The price for the targets have gone up to $89.95 and $99.95.

Zombie Industries' targets ooze paint and come apart graphically when each bullet hits them. Trust me on this. The website provides YouTube videos to demonstrate what happens to the targets when they are shot: hunks of synthetic flesh fall off and faces and torsos are obliterated. The effect is haunting and disturbing. I felt nauseated as I watched one of the videos. These zombies never stood a chance. They weren't supposed to.

Two 3D zombie targets, "Rocky" and "Alexa," brought negative attention to Zombie Industries in 2013. Previously on their website, Zombie Industries described Rocky "as a fighter from Detroit," who received his "nickname" after "a few matches left him rutted in the head." Heroically, Rocky staved off an undead attack, but later succumbed to bites. Yet his newly zombified state shouldn't fool you: "Be warned, Rocky is HIGHLY dangerous due to his quick wit and strength…. He was last seen screaming something like 'Zombie Industries believes in America!' That we do." The website now offers no back story, just a production description and the guarantee that Rocky was "made in the U.S.A. by non-infected workers."

The controversy surrounding the green-skinned Rocky was that for some he resembles President Barack Obama. (I can still see some of the possible similarities.) *BuzzFeed* reported that the possible resemblance of the Rocky model to Obama led the National Rifle Association (NRA) to ban that model from their exhibit hall at the 2013 NRA Convention. Zombie Industries displayed Rocky for two days at the convention before removing the model at the NRA's request. A booth worker told *BuzzFeed* that the NRA feared "a liberal reporter would come by and start bitching." When *BuzzFeed* asked if the resemblance was intentional, another worker noted, "Let's just say I gave my Republican father one for Christmas."[8]

Yet Zombie Industries CEO Roger Davis told MSN news that the NRA did not ask them to remove Rocky from their booth. Instead, the booth sold out of Rocky zombies, which is why the model was suddenly off the display. Moreover, Davis took issue with the claim that Rocky looked like Obama; rather, Rocky *was* supposed to look like an African-American man but the target was not geared to resemble a certain person.[9] I guess that was supposed to make us feel better, but it really doesn't.

On Zombie Industries' webpage, the company placed the blame for this controversy on liberal news outlets. A front-page announcement declared, "Don't let the liberal media allow your imagination run wild with silly ideas...there is no political motivation...we hate ALL zombies." Supposedly all zombies, not just ones that looked like the first Black president. More importantly, the target manufacturer emphasized that just like the zombie virus does not discriminate among human victims, neither does the company. Davis explained to MSN news, "Zombie Industries does not discriminate on the basis of race, religion, or gender. Our zombies represent the current demographic in America today."[10] Supposedly, creating zombies of different races and genders was a way to be inclusive. But I remain unconvinced because the targets draw heavily from stereotypes (remember the terrorist target). Stereotypes shouldn't be confused with being inclusive.

The company turned the controversy into a promotion—if shoppers entered DEBATE at checkout, they would have received 30% off their entire purchase.

While Davis attempted to distance Rocky from the claims that he looked like Obama, a YouTube review of the target purposely conjured the likeness. The video review, which has since been removed by the user, renamed the target "Barry." The white reviewer shot the target with arrows and then two separate guns while his preschool age son looked on. He enthusiastically noted that "Barry never stood a chance" against the twelve-gauge shotgun. Who would?

In addition to the news coverage about the Rocky target, the "Alexa" zombie also stirred up a controversy for the company. This target was supposedly an ex-girlfriend, who, according to the Zombie Industries website in 2013, had "a wicked mean streak" and a "nasty disposition." She was originally named, "The Ex-Girlfriend," but her name was later changed to Alexa. Unlike Rocky, who had green skin, the original Alexa target had fair skin splattered with blood. Her pink bra was visible under her white tank top. Simply put, this target appeared much more human than the rest of the zombified targets. This difference from the male zombie targets seems intentional, as their skin colors range from green to grey.

What proved more disturbing were the comments on the Alexa product page at Zombie Industries' website, a page that no longer exists at all. One male commenter describes the target as "this Zombie Bitch" who reminded him of "a girl he knew in high school." The *Huffington Post* noted that one commenter wrote, "The dark haired one looks like my bitch ex-wife, who I HATE! I can't wait to shoot her face off for taking my shit."[11] This particular comment was removed from the page, though the other comments remained as long as the page was up. Most of the reviews of Alexa were five star reviews by male reviewers, though two female reviewers did give the product one star reviews.

Zombie Industries' website stated, "To discriminate against Women by not having them represented in our product selection would be just plain sexist." To exclude women might appear sexist, but the description of, and the reaction to, the Alexa target was rife with misogyny. Many feared that this target encouraged men to enact violent fantasies about women using guns. After all, in the U.S., men are 90% of the perpetrators of domestic violence and women are 85% of all domestic violence victims. Every day, around four women a day lose their lives to domestic violence.[12] When an abuser has access to a gun, according to the Giffords Law Center, it becomes five times more likely that a woman will be killed. In the U.S., intimate partners shoot and kill 600 women a year.[13]

As I read the reviews of Alexa, I couldn't separate the reality of women as victims of domestic abuse and the danger that guns pose to them with the reviewers' excitement about shooting the sole female target. Rather, these men were eager to shoot a target who represented women that they imagined had wronged them. Alexa became a conduit for their rage, a literal target for their desire for vengeance as well as their frustration and hate for living and breathing women. Several petitions encouraged Amazon to remove Alexa from their site and emphasized that this target made violence against women seem like a joke. Amazon removed the target from their store. Later, Zombie Industries did as well. There are no female targets on the site anymore.

However, I keep coming back to how CEO Davis claimed that the goal of Zombie Industries was to provide fun, entertaining targets that promote gun safety. Shooting a target must be better than shooting a person, right? No actual people are being harmed by a bleeding target. It is just harmless fun. Isn't it? I remain unconvinced.

Despite Davis's claims, the targets suggest something else: the unhindered glee of destroying zombies that promotes a particular version of acceptable violence. Anyone can become a target as long as they are zombified. But the line of separation between zombies and humans seems murky here. These zombies appear too reminiscent of humans, and they allow violence directed toward a zombie president or ex-girlfriend to be marketed as fun and safe. I am not convinced that it can be either. While the stated goal of the Alexa target is to include zombified women among the male-dominated targets, I can't help but think of the argument between the Long Island couple that ended with gun violence against a young woman. Real life often mimics fantasy, or maybe, fantasy is dress rehearsal for real life—for good or ill.

I have so many questions for the men who buy this target: Does shooting a target that looks like your ex-girlfriend help you? I seriously doubt it. Or does it just encourage you to dwell in negative emotions about her? Probably. Why would you purchase one in the first place? Is it revenge? What do these targets do for you? Are they a stand-in for a woman or the women you claim have hurt you? Are the targets a way for you to imagine hurting them?

When I look at Alexa, I see all the negative ways in which women are viewed in American culture. Objectification. Sexualization. Violence. Alexa is literally an object. Her bra is exposed, and her body oozes and falls apart when shot. This does not suggest a move away from sexism or violence against women but rather a capitalistic exploitation of it. The fragility of this target, and all the others, highlights the fragility of human bodies. We can be so easily broken, destroyed, and maimed. Watching the destruction of Zombie Industries targets makes me uneasy because of the comparison.

Bodies come apart, and the lauded realism makes it hard for me to look. What is the relationship between zombies and humans? What are zombies stand-ins for? Are they a representation of humans that we don't like or actively want to harm? Who are the people we make into zombies?

This violence against zombies dramatizes the close relationship of the pop culture monster to the American culture of violence. Paying attention to how some Americans prepare for zombies reveals the presence and perception of gun violence in the U.S. In zombie media and zombie prep, guns appear as both offensive and defensive, guarantors of the peace and the causes of unrest. They prove necessary. They are stockpiled. They are glorified. Americans simultaneously love and hate them; we are ambivalent. Some legislate for stricter control while others seek protection of their so-called cherished rights. The ubiquity of guns appears to be the unquestioned given.

Guns, controlled or not, appear here to stay. And gun violence is ordinary and common. In 2010, over twelve thousand Americans were killed by guns. In 2019, that number rose to over 15,200. We live in an age of mass shootings. Since the Newtown shooting in 2012, there have been 2,442 mass shootings in the U.S. Newtown was supposed to be the moment in which Americans decided "never again," but that clearly wasn't the case.

In fact, since 2013, there's only been one calendar week (in 2014) without a mass shooting.[14] The Covid-19 pandemic and the requirements to shelter in place might mean we go longer than a week without a mass shooting, but there is no guarantee that mass shootings will stop forever.

We also live in an age of police killings. In 2019, *The Washington Post* reports that the police shot and killed over one thousand people in 2019.[15] That was five years after white police officer Darren Wilson shot and killed Michael Brown, an eighteen-year-old Black man, in Ferguson, Missouri. That was also six years after George Zimmerman's acquittal for the murder of Trayvon Martin, a seventeen-year-old Black student, spurred the beginning of the Black Lives Matter movement. In 2019, a study in the *Proceedings of the National Academies of Science*s found that Black men and boys "face the highest risk of being killed by police." During their lives, Black men have a one in one thousand chance of being killed in an encounter with the police.[16] Videos of police officers brutalizing and killing Black people appear on the news and in social media, autoplaying the loss of life in a terrible loop.

Of course, there aren't only videos, but eyewitness accounts of some police officers' casual violence toward Black people. Police officers are rarely punished for these killings, despite public outcry and demands for justice.

The news coverage of the mass shootings and police killings garner national attention for a little while, but their ubiquity seems to make them a little less newsworthy every day. Guns, which are often used in both, appear as an unremarkable part of tragic, predictable events and preventable deaths.

While guns might seem unremarkable in some ways, Americans largely perceive that gun violence has increased over the years. And yet, there was a 49% decline in gun violence from 1993 until 2011.[17] But that perception of increasing gun violence persists even now. A 2019 PBS Newshour/Marist poll showed that many Americans continue to assume that gun violence is on the rise. Most of those surveyed believed the rate of murder by guns was higher now than twenty-five years ago. This belief, however, remains incorrect. The numbers for murder rates with guns are still not as high as they were in 1993.[18] In 1993, there were over 18,000 gun-related murders, but by 2017, the number dropped to just over 10,900.[19] Gun violence might worry us, but not enough for many American politicians to take it seriously enough to prevent.

Mass shootings and police killings continue to be painfully ordinary. They are tragedies, but there are Americans who refuse to give up their attachment to guns, no matter how deadly they prove to be. It should be no surprise, then, that visions of the zombie apocalypse still rely so heavily on firepower and weaponry. If guns are a dominant component of American culture, then pop culture merely reflects those norms. And the zombie apocalypse indulges in a fantasy that guns can protect us from any threat, if only our aim remains true. The doomsday preppers have stockpiled guns and other weapons to be ready for any disaster on the horizon. They hoarded guns because they feared their guns might be taken away at any moment during the Obama presidency.

These preppers and other Americans wanted guns so they would be prepared for any threats that came their way; zombies were just one of many terrifying fates that they planned for. However, weapons and ammo made supposedly for killing zombies could eliminate any human threat, too. This is why I worry about the relationship between zombies and guns. Gun violence directed first at fictional monsters can easily slip into violence against humans. Training to kill zombies could lead to the actual harm of living, breathing humans. While Zombie Industries might have insisted that their oozing zombie targets were all in good fun, I'm not sure that they were or are now. I think back to the comments about the Alexa zombie target, and all the men that purchased and reviewed it. They were excited to destroy Alexa because she reminded them of the women in their lives that supposedly did them wrong. They wanted to shoot her in the face because they wanted to shoot these living, breathing women in the face too. The line between fiction and reality was blurred, not distinct. They wanted their violent fantasies to come true. So, the belief in the reality of the zombie apocalypse can condone violence now and in the future and glorify the power of guns to eliminate any threat, monster or human. The zombie apocalypse is not a future we should prepare for; it's a blood soaked one that no one should look forward to. But so many of us still do.

AFTERWORD: "YOU'VE GOT SOME RED ON YOU."
Looking at Zombies, Looking at Ourselves

The zombies are here, and they're not going away, but they're not the story.
—Mira Grant, *Feed*

In the fall of 2011, one of my former students from my Apocalypse in American Culture course emailed me to tell me about a Facebook event that might interest me. She was right; it did. The event was the "Zombie Apocalypse," scheduled for December 22, 2012, notably a day after the supposed Mayan Apocalypse. According to the event's page, 1,074,824 people signed up to attend, 157,455 offered "maybe attending," and 615,478 politely declined their invitation to a gun-toting, gore-filled end.[1] (I accepted my invitation, if you are curious.)

The event site proclaimed:

The time is finally set. The day of the dead is coming, so make sure you have your Zombie Survival Plan ready. Many people are concerned about December 21, 2012, the alleged end of the world. This is just a ploy to hide the real day of reckoning, December 22, 2012, THE ZOMBIE APOCALYPSE! Grab your sawed-off shotgun, baseball bat and your running shoes and be prepared to kill or be killed! Oh, and by the way, you've got some red on you.[2]

The Facebook page for the event was filled with helpful hints for zombie killing, the almost required comparison and contrast of preferred weaponry, general excitement over the possibility of zombies, and a keen desire to do harm to these monsters. Months after the supposed end of the world via zombies, folks lamented that the end did not occur and suggested new dates. Prophecy doesn't match reality, and apocalyptic disappointment set in again. Now, years later, I wonder if the participants even remember the event or how they RSVPed. Is it a vague memory or does it feel like a lost opportunity? The page no longer exists, as if it were never quite there to begin with.

I'm still fascinated by the back and forth dialogue between participants on the page about why someone would take this made-up event so seriously. In the comments, an occasional poster decried the loss of energy and time wasted on this far-fetched doomsday. There were more important things to pay attention to, right? Global unrest, hunger, terror, and war, just to name a few. Attendees fired back that the zombie apocalypse was fun. It was harmless really. It was just *fun* to imagine devastation, destruction, and ruin of our world. Imagining and planning for an improbable catastrophe didn't necessarily cancel out anyone's attention to global or domestic problems.

Fun, fun, fun, they commented over and over again.

When compared to the bleakness of zombie apocalypse portrayal in film, television, and fiction, the palpable excitement on a long-gone Facebook page might seem a bit disconcerting. Paired with zombie emergency preparedness, attacks involving cannibalism, zombie preppers, and oozing 3D zombie targets, this event seemed sadly typical to me. Of course an event like this *would* exist. Of course it would. For many, zombies are a whole lot of fun, even if they tend to end civilization in popular culture. At this point, I doubt that any of you readers are surprised that some, perhaps many, Americans like imagining how to destroy zombies in novel and grotesque ways. I haven't been surprised by this for at least a decade now. What continues to stump me is how the undead apocalypse remains desirable, laughable, entertaining, or even joyful. I still somehow miss the punchline. I still don't think it is a joke.

Adding the long-ago Facebook event to all the other examples in this book makes the zombie apocalypse appear not as fun, but instead as commentary about how we view humanity in our often-brutal present. Violent fantasy echoes and amplifies an equally violent but seemingly safe reality. Violence is always with us, even as we try to overlook it. Sure, zombies are dangerous, but so are we. In zombie movies, novels and TV shows, humans are just as likely as the shuffling monsters to destroy, consume, or maim our fellow human beings. George Romero's classic *Night of the Living Dead* (1968) made this clear. Humans, in our potential for cruelty and violence, are the real threat. By preparing for and getting ready to kill zombies, we push onto the monster all the things we hope we are not, but also those things that we are.

Zombies are the bearers of the end because they have no agency, no humanity, and no final end in sight. They are relentless, hungry, and inescapable. They are near and present death. They press forward without soul or mind, and often missing various body parts. They do not stop trying to destroy us. But they can't help it. Destroying us is what zombies do. The fantasy of the zombie apocalypse plays out the end of humanity again and again in more and more bleak incarnations. In every rendering, the boundary between human and zombie becomes muddier and muddier, as humans become as unfeeling and callous as the ever-hungry, never-satiated monster. We shovel all those terrible traits of humanity onto them, and then, we kill them to cover up all of our transgressions. In preparing for monsters, I can't help but wonder if we become them.

Do you remember the discussion of whether to shoot your infected child or not? Do you cringe at the thought of an oozing Alexa target with chunks of her body missing and blood splattered across her tank top? Do you imagine what it might be like to have your face chewed on? Do you ponder the horror of surviving a senseless act of violence and becoming a media spectacle? Do you wonder about caches of weapons and civilian militias? Do you pause and wonder how Jessica Gelderman recovered from a gunshot wound? I do. These stories stick with me, and I cannot shed them. They make me worry. They make me cynical. The lines between zombie and human seem too easy to ignore or to dismiss. Fantasy and reality have become dangerously intertwined, if they were ever really separate to begin with.

Zombies become the reason for humanity's fictionalized and supposedly destined end because they showcase how fragile humans actually are, with or without crisis. When zombies appear in film and books or on TV, society collapses oh-so-quickly. The tenuous bonds that hold us together are not frayed but broken, and we turn on one another. Yes, we kill zombies, but we harm and kill each other too. In these zombie stories, all it takes is the beginning of a catastrophe to make us our worst selves who rely on violence to get what we want at the cost of other people.

What the persistent belief in the zombie apocalypse might truly teach us is the centrality of violence in American culture and our familiarity with destroyed human bodies. The pervasive millennial zombies resemble the corpses that litter our actual world. Famine. Disease. War. Terror. Old Age. Young Age. Accidents. Guns. Natural disasters. Death comes for us all; it's a tie that binds us together. We live, and we die. Corpses, however, do not resurrect or walk, but we bear them with us. While we analyze which weapon would be more fun—gun or baseball bat—to harm a zombie, we become more comfortable with the destruction of ordinary folks. We casually accept harm and violence. Violence becomes a mundane part of daily life that doesn't garner our attention unless it's something out of the ordinary that can be played up for clicks on websites or capture the viewer's attention in the 24-hour news cycle.

Perhaps I am being too harsh, too dreary, or too melodramatic. Maybe walking corpses become a method to manage those who haunt us but aren't seen. Maybe they help us handle all the kinds of things that are beyond our control. Yet, the specter of violence lingers, and as Max Brooks reminds us, there is only one way to kill a zombie—but with humans the possibilities are endless.

All of this is to say that whether the zombie apocalypse is real or not is the wrong question. It is much less important if the undead doomsday is real and more important to consider what participating in these fantasies leads to. Cultural theorist Edward Ingebretsen reminds us that monsters set up the limits for humanity by warning us of the boundaries that we shouldn't cross.[3] They also become blank canvases for what we fear and value. We place our burdens on monsters instead of taking care of them ourselves.

Zombies, then, demonstrate the reality of American fears about disaster (natural or human-made), disease and epidemic, the government's stability, terrorism, and gun control. More broadly, these monsters suggest the value of apocalypticism, fatalism, and violence in American culture. Preparing for an end by zombies reflects a deep ambivalence about our political culture, civic life, and the future of our nation. If the end is the future that awaits us, why imagine a better world and work to make it a reality? If the end is truly unstoppable, why would we try to fix anything? We all should just give up and prep for the inevitable doomsday with supplies, gear, and guns. Zombies might be just fantasy, but they have real stakes. Preparation for these monsters allows many Americans to participate in a vision of a different world in which the current social order disappears, and only some survive.

Rather than assuming that fear and violence don't have to be our future, the zombie apocalypse claims a perilous and awful future is our only option. It's a future, in which we tear each other apart instead of trying to build something better for all of us. The possibilities are only horrifying and never hopeful. When I hear my daughter and son say, "Zombies aren't real," I want to be reassured. To agree with them. To proclaim that fantasy can't be reality. To place zombies solely in fiction. To ignore the dangers of wanting the world to end. To overlook the violence that the fictional apocalypses have wrought.

Saying zombies aren't real doesn't make it so.

There are still Americans who believe the zombie apocalypse could be real. They are working to make the possibility into a reality, through prepping and purchasing guns and ammo supposedly for use on only monsters. They want to transform *if* into *when*. They want the bloody future, even if it means most of us won't survive. And yet, there are also those who rely on the zombie apocalypse to do cultural work like convince us that emergency preparedness matters, that training for unknown threats is important, or to make sense of violent attacks that are just senseless. Their efforts can sometimes help us but they also hold us back. Their use of monsters can become just another excuse to dehumanize certain people and excuse violence. They all use the zombie apocalypse to create the world they want, whether the rest of us want that world or not. It's about them, not about us. And we need more people to consider what's best for all of us rather than focus on their own interests, desires, and wants and how they might only get these things through force and harm.

So, yes, the zombies are everywhere. I can't avoid them, and neither can you. Are you ready to face them? Because you need to. Zombies, like all monsters, are our creations, but they are also projections of ourselves. Monsters represent our worries, our fears, our violence, and all of our other terrible traits that we would rather pretend we didn't have. They are a mirror that we try not to look into. Zombies are our mirror, right now, and we can't look away. We can't. But, zombies aren't the problem, not really. We are. If we take a hard look at zombies, we have to take a hard look at ourselves. And maybe, just maybe, we'll decide that we don't like what we see and that we can change. Maybe then we'll begin to build a better, more humane world rather than wait eagerly for the end of one.

INTERVIEW IN THEOFANTASTIQUE

"Kelly J. Baker: *The Zombies Are Coming!*"
TheoFantastisque, June 14, 2013.
By John Morehead

For a while now I have been following the work of my friend and colleague, Kelly J. Baker, and she recently shared a copy of her new book with me on zombies and apocalypticism. The book is titled *The Zombies Are Coming!: The Realities of the Zombie Apocalypse in American Culture* (Bondfire Books, 2013), and I highly recommend a download for anyone interested in probing the zombie in more depth.

Kelly is also the author of *Gospel According to the Klan: The KKK's Appeal to Protestant America, 1915-1930* (University Press of Kansas, 2011).

Kelly made time in her busy schedule to discuss aspects of her recent book.

TheoFantastique: As a scholar studying American religion and apocalypticism, when and how did zombies come across your radar and bring both of these areas together for you?

Kelly Baker: My first brush with the zombie apocalypse occurred while I was teaching a class called The Apocalypse in American Culture, which pretty much covered end-times theologies in *Left Behind*, *The Turner Diaries*, UFOlogy, environmental activism, Heaven's Gate, Branch Davidians, and pop culture more broadly. What I discovered is that my students were far more interested in talking about zombies and the end than any other topic. They loved zombies. They recommended books, films, and graphic novels, and they wanted to strategize for a zombie apocalypse with me. I tried to convince them that I am no help when it comes to preparing for doomsday.

This passion my students had for a particular type of end made me very curious about zombies. Why zombies? Why did walking corpses have so much appeal? Why were zombies so popular? And why was this monster most often paired with the end of days? My students caused me to steer my research away from doomsday theologies into the cultural representations of zombie apocalypse and their possible consequences. I would have never imagined that I would write about zombies, but these monsters prove to be a fascinating case study that I can't walk away from.

TheoFantastique: One of the main threads of your book's thesis is the importance of apocalypticism in American thought. How might elements of the Christian "end-times" mythos continue to inform this, and how might this connect even to something as seemingly secular as the zombie?

Kelly Baker: The apocalypse is always with us. Americans find the end lurking around all kinds of corners, and we consume ends in theology, entertainment, and politics. Impending doom emerges as a familiar narrative that gets recreated, reimagined, and reassessed in both American past and present. So, yes, I do think apocalypticism is crucial component in American thought and life. More importantly, Christian end-times visions dominated American history and influenced the secular forms of apocalypticism, in which the world is torn apart not by divine force but by human hands. Religious and secular doomsdays are enmeshed in one another in ways that we might not expect. Much of the reason for this is that the apocalypse is a religious genre that voices the corruptness of a current moment and a hope for a redemptive future. Secular adaptations of doomsday cannot get away from its religious roots, even though they might try, but they are often more fatalistic in tone. Redemption disappears. The religious moorings of apocalypticism almost haunt secular renditions. Lingering traces of Christian end-times theologies pop up again and again.

What I am interested in, then, is the assumed secularity of the zombie and how the zombie apocalypse gets presented as somehow not, or even anti-, religious. Most often I get asked how a religious studies scholar can write about zombies or monsters, and I point out that I have plenty to write about depending upon one's definition of religion. With my flip answer, I am not trying to say that these monsters are inherently religious, but these monsters become a way to communicate what is human and what is not.

David Chidester defines religion as being human in a human place, and I think that zombies give us a way to think about the limits of what we want to call humanity. Additionally, I find the zombie's relationship with apocalypticism utterly fascinating because it suggests that the boundaries we might imagine between religious and secular are neither firm nor unyielding. The merger of zombies and the end provide an excellent case study for thinking about how doomsday changes to meet the needs of our modern world as well as how we define "religion" and "human" as a categories in a supposedly post-secular age.

TheoFantastique: I remember being fascinated by many of the events in pop culture that you reference, such as the CDC's use of zombies in disaster preparedness, and the panic among some segments of the population about alleged "zombie attacks." Christopher Partridge has said the West now features "fact-fiction reversals" where aspects of fictional pop culture cross the blurred line into perceptions of reality. What do you see as contributing to this boundary blurring and crossover with this iconic monster of the day?

Kelly Baker: I wonder if those boundaries that separate fiction and reality were ever really boundaries at all. I am not sure that there is something about our particular moment that leads to "blurring," but rather that the imagination creeps up on us when we least expect it. Sometimes unreality seems more believable than reality, and sometimes we just wish that reality contained more of the fantastic. My daughter is four, and she inhabits a world of enchantment and possibility, in which fairies can be real, Jack Frost guards children, and the Sandman brings good dreams. It is a lovely space that makes clear distinctions between good and evil with required happy endings. Sometimes, I envy the possibility and enchantment that she sees everywhere, but most often I want her to enjoy what the imagination can offer.

The ambiguity of real life often lacks the order and ethics of fantasy. Maybe we want that possibility and clarity even if we need a bleak zombie apocalypse to bring it. Maybe we still want to believe in monsters in a world that seemingly lacks mystery, where everything seems known or knowable. Maybe the arrival of zombies will prove that what we envision our lives to be are not what they actually are.

TheoFantastique: One particularly troubling aspect of your book is the discussion of the connection of American gun culture to the zombie. Can you provide a few examples of how this plays out? And from your research, might the living dead and dehumanized zombie through the prevalence of it in film, television and video games contribute to this connection?

Kelly Baker: The association between zombies and guns is one that troubles me too. To kill a zombie, the preferred weapon of choice appears to be a gun, and we see many examples of this in film, television, and video games. My husband tends to point out the uncanny aim of human survivors in *The Walking Dead*; guns become equated with safety and protection. There's also a glorification of the murder of the undead without much engagement with the ethical concerns in zombie media. The relationship of fictional violence to real violence is complicated, and studies, particularly of video games, come to contradictory conclusions. What worries me is the glee that destroying zombies produces. What are the consequences? How does the destruction of zombies prime us for other forms of destruction and violence?

Crucially, imaginary monsters can lead to actual violence. Just last week, two Arkansas teenage boys were playing a zombie game, and one shot the other in the shoulder with a .40 caliber pistol. In the book, I discuss another incident where a man shot his girlfriend over an argument about *The Walking Dead* as well as the marketing of zombie guns, ammunition, and targets. Why are we so eager and excited to eradicate them? Why does zombification make destruction of human bodies okay? This process of dehumanization makes me nervous about the consumption and participation in zombie media. What does killing these monsters do for us? Cultural theorist Edward Ingebretsen notes that we "stake" the monster to define what is human. I just wonder what type of humanity we define in every zombie kill.

INTERVIEW IN RELIGION BULLETIN

"*The Zombies Are Coming!*" An Interview with Kelly J. Baker on the Zombie Apocalypse
Religion Bulletin, July 31, 2013
By Philip L. Tite

Recently, our colleague here at the *Bulletin*, Kelly Baker, published a short book entitled, *The Zombies Are Coming! The Realities of the Zombie Apocalypse in American Culture* (Bondfire Books, 2013). In this readable and engaging book, we are thrown into the eclectic realm of zombies in American culture(s). Rather than seeing zombies as a fad or an entertaining escape from reality, Baker draws up into the web of imagination where zombies become sites of political, social, and ideological contestation. Yet the book is directed at a general audience. In reading through this book, I thought that it would be good to introduce readers of the *Bulletin*'s blog to this work and, more importantly, the implications of a scholar sharing her research through such a work.

Kelly was kind enough to agree to an interview on her book.

Philip Tite: Can you tell us something about your target audience? This work seems to reach out to the non-academic. Does this tell us something about your view on the function of scholarship?

Kelly Baker: I've always wanted to write something that my family would be interested in reading. My sisters and mom attempted to read my Klan book, but they didn't finish it. The academic monograph does not captivate a larger audience, which is fine because it is not really supposed to. The book, then, is my attempt to reach beyond academic audiences to a larger general readership. *The Zombies Are Coming!* is my attempt to engage not only my family, but also anybody else who is interested in zombies and the apocalypse. I am bringing my research in a different form to different conversation partners, which I find very exciting. Currently, my aunt and uncle are reading it, and my youngest sister read and liked it.

For me, the book becomes a vehicle to move my scholarship beyond the limits of the academy into the public square.

More and more, I think that we, academics, do ourselves a grave disservice by limiting our scholarship to our peers. I constantly ask myself what my scholarship should accomplish and interrogate the *why* of what I do. Yes, I want to continue conversations about my research topics with other experts, but I consider this only part of what scholars should do. We should also be able to take what we know, research, and write into more public venues and communicate what we do clearly and coherently. We need to explain what is at stake in our research to the general public. Otherwise, we allow pundits to control public discourse. Converting the complexity of what we study might seem like an insurmountable challenge, but it isn't. If you can't translate your project into something more easily accessible to a broader audience, then something has gone wrong. We deal in complexity, but that doesn't mean we get to hide behind it.

Philip Tite: Do you think that other religious studies scholars will benefit from this book? What do you hope they will take away from this book?

Kelly Baker: Yes, I hope that other religious studies scholars will benefit from this book, especially the discussion of apocalypticism's central role in American culture and the importance of zombies in popular culture and public life. There's a tendency in both media and scholarly accounts to represent apocalypticism as fringe and/or marginal. The coverage of apocalypticism tends to represent practitioners as "crazy" while also underplaying how many Americans participate in doomsday belief and practice. Crucially, this ignores the power of apocalypticism as a rhetoric tool and mode of interpretation for many Americans. Moreover, what does it mean that a religious system, apocalypticism, appears so readily in popular culture? Why does apocalypticism work so well in film, television, music, fiction, and now social media? What can attention to the prominence of doomsday tell us about the current moment and past moments in American history? What happens when we turn our analysis to apocalypticism's popularity in American culture? What do we learn?

Zombies, then, emerge as only one particular example of pop apocalypticism with dark visions of humanity's future. More and more, religious studies scholars study the relationship of religions to their various monsters, particularly Timothy Beal, W. Scott Poole, John Morehead, and Kim Paffenroth, as well as the importance of horror to religious systems with Edward Ingebretsen's *At Stake* and Jason Bivins' *The Religion of Fear* as the best examples. My work on zombies, then, carries forward the conversations on religion, horror, and monstrosity. We can learn much from what we fear.

Philip Tite: You also chose to publish your book through a very different venue than normal book publishing. Can you comment on that choice, why you think it is an advantage for this particular book?

Kelly Baker: This project is not a traditional print monograph. Rather, *The Zombies Are Coming!* is an ebook only, so this format was really an experiment for me. I wanted to see how writing and publishing of an ebook differed from my previous experiences with the monograph and how this electronic format might prove beneficial to publicizing my scholarship. When Bondfire Books approached me about an extended article (around 50 pages) about the zombie apocalypse, I jumped at the opportunity to write something more akin to cultural criticism based on my research for a general audience.

Part of the reason I found the ebook appealing was the quick turnaround. Since I was writing about events from the past couple of years, the ebook format allowed me to present my work much more rapidly than a traditional monograph. Importantly, this allowed me to think and write about zombies in a shorter form that is easier to market to a broader audience. Additionally, I appreciated the ability to experiment with my writing for different readers. For example, my fabulous editor, Patton Dodd, urged me to think very carefully about not only my style of writing but also my *voice*. Rather than the disembodied voice that characterizes much of academic writing, my voice is much more collegial and personal (and, I hope, engaging). I am visible in the ebook in a way that I am not in *Gospel According to the Klan*. There is certain vulnerability in including yourself as a part of the narrative, which might appear subjective and out of place in the monograph (though this style appears more readily in ethnography). I find this empowering and useful. And now, my academic work more often reflects my preferred voice.

Philip Tite: Are "zombies" a subject for religious studies research? It falls outside the norm of what we study. Have there been any reactions so far to the data you study?

Kelly Baker: Ah, the "how is this religion?" question rears its ugly head. (Well, maybe, not ugly, but annoying, persistent, typical, or familiar head) I will admit that zombies do fall outside the "norm" of what religious studies scholars expect "religion" to be. But, I wouldn't be happy unless I was pressing the boundaries of what religious studies can and can't do. My research, for better or worse, challenges assumptions about what is/isn't religion. My first book examined the 1920s Klan to demonstrate the centrality of Protestantism to white supremacy, and many scholars interrogated whether the Klan could be "religious." If the Klan is hard to imagine as religious, then zombies are beyond the pale.

Much of the reaction about the Klan and zombies comes from assumptions about what is properly religion, and I've already had my say about this in my piece on evidence for the *Bulletin for the Study of Religion*. Why are some scholars so avidly policing "religion"? What does this tell us about how "religion" is defined and deployed?

Frankly, I think that it shows that some still buy into a tired "I know religion when I see it" that fits neatly with a world religions paradigm, an emphasis on theology and institutions, or the common Protestantized definition of religion as belief. The living dead seem to not fit well with theses characterizations. Resurrected corpses, in this instance, become a problem.

When I use zombies as data, it causes discomfort because it suggests that maybe religion is not as familiar or as easily identifiable as we think it is. Maybe we would have to admit that J.Z. Smith is right about religion being constructed by scholars in every use. Maybe we would have to note that our interlocutors also construct religion in every utterance of the word.

Philip Tite: I noticed that the book is a bit light on the theorization side of the analysis, which I'm assuming is a deliberate choice given the target audience. Yet, a recurring theme that hit me was that "zombies" are not divorced from broader political, social, and economic debates. Could you comment a bit on this point?

Kelly Baker: Side swiping my readers with theory would not have been the best choice. They probably don't care if I find Avery Gordon, Edward Ingebretsen, Julia Kristeva, or Kathleen Stewart remarkably helpful to my research on zombies. These scholars undergird my approach to monsters, but the ebook was more documentary and less theoretical. Of course, zombies are enmeshed in political, social, and economic debates because the rhetoric of the zombie appears in all these arenas. Zombie voters, Obama zombies, Tea Party zombies, zombie banks, zombie cell phone users, zombie consumers, and students as zombies are only some of the ways the undead appear in national and personal debates. Zombies are excellent signifiers; they can represent almost anything. Thus, they become the vehicles to describe anything that one wants to claim is mindless and destructive.

Philip Tite: Why is there such a fascination with zombies these days? Is this just a fad that will fade away or is this fascination something deeper?

Kelly Baker: Why wouldn't you be fascinated by the living dead? They shamble, ooze, moan, and fall apart. Isn't that what we all aspire to? Likely not. There is much speculation about why Americans are fascinated by zombies that often hinges on escapism. I find escapism to be a wholly unsatisfying answer because it feels too easy and dismissive. It is clear that zombies work well as a metaphor for the early twenty-first century. There is a complicated answer as to why that I don't fully understand yet, so I want to avoid the temptation to pin the zombie's popularity on a possible answer. Postmodernity, global war, neoliberalism, racism, misogyny, secularism, supernaturalism, and gun violence all tie into the zombie's pervasiveness, but the *why* still remains elusive.

Zombies could be a fad, but their duration from the 1930s until today suggests that maybe the zombie will outlast other monsters. They are the living dead, after all. They resurrect in different forms in different times and places from "voodoo" zombies to cannibalistic monsters to fast infected humans to introspective corpses. It makes me wonder if all that binds zombies together is the label affixed to them.

Philip Tite: Finally, are you a zombie?

Kelly Baker: No comment.

NOTES

EPIGRAPH

1. Edward Ingebretsen, *Maps of Heaven, Maps of Hell: Religious Terror as Memory from Puritans to Stephen King*, Sharp, 1996.
2. Rebecca Solnit, *Hope in the Dark: Untold Histories, Wild Possibilities*, Haymarket Books, 2004.

FOREWORD: "EXTREME ZOMBIE ACTIVITY"

1. Stephen King, *Danse Macabre*, Hodder & Stoughton, 2006.
2. Susan Leighton, "Power Outage in Florida Generates 'Extreme Zombie Activity' Warning," *Fansided*, August 5, 2018 and Ed Mazza, "Power Outage Triggers 'Extreme Zombie Activity' Alert in Florida City," *Huffington Post*, May 22, 2008.
3. Max Brooks, *The Zombie Survival Guide: Complete Protection from the Undead*, Del Rey, 2003.
4. "Fossil Reveals 48-million-year History of Zombie Ants," *Science Daily*, August 18, 2010.
5. Solnit, *Hope in the Dark*.
6. David Edelstein, "Zombies in the Time of Ebola: Why We Need Horror Movies Now More than Ever," *Vulture*, October 21, 2014.

1. INTRODUCTION: "MOMMY, ZOMBIES AREN'T REAL."

1. Geoff Pevere, "Zombies: Why This Pop-Culture Phenomenon Will Not Die," *The Globe and Mail*, Jan. 31, 2013.

2. Lev Grossman, "Zombies Are the New Vampires," *Time*, April 20, 2009.
3. Pevere, "Zombies: Why This Pop-Culture Phenomenon Will Not Die."
4. "Nation's Zombie Craze Brings Dead to Life," MyFoxTampaBay.Com, February 26, 2013.
5. Daniel W. Drezner, "Night of the Living Wonks," *Foreign Policy*, June 15, 2010.
6. "Researcher: Zombie Fads Peak When Society in Unhappy," *Associated Press*, March 10, 2013.
7. "'The Walking Dead' Hits TV History, But Falls From 2016 Finale In Live+3," *Deadline*, April 7, 2017.
8. "Zombies Worth Over $5 Billion to Economy," *24/7 Wall Street*, October 25, 2011.
9. Jeffrey Jerome Cohen, "Monster Culture (Seven Theses)," in *Monster Theory: Reading Culture*, edited by Jeffrey Jerome Cohen, University of Minnesota Press, 1996.
10. Cohen, "Monster Culture (Seven Theses)."
11. "4 Reasons the Zombie Apocalypse Would Benefit Humanity in the Long Run," *Cracked*, no longer available.

2. "APOCALYPSE OBSESSION."

1. Kelly J. Murphy, "The World IS (Always) About to End, No Zombies Required," *Religion Dispatches*, March 5, 2015.
2. Nicole Saidi, "Be honest: Apocalypse seems kind of exciting, in a way," *CNN*, December 7, 2012.
3. Natalie Wolchover, "NASA Crushes 2012 Mayan Apocalypse Claims," *Scientific American*, March 9, 2012.
4. Bill Whitaker, "How Harold Camping Marketed the Rapture," *CBS News*, May 20, 2011.
5. Nicole Saidi, "Be honest: Apocalypse seems kind of exciting, in a way."

6. Kelsey Piper, "Doomsday clock creators: 'We're playing Russian roulette with humanity,'" *Vox*, January 24, 2019.
7. Arthur Williamson, *Apocalypse Then: Prophecy and the Making of the Modern World*, Praeger, 2008.
8. "Startling Numbers of Americans Believe World Now in the 'End Times,'" *Religion News Service*, September 11, 2013.
9. Ronald Bailey, "Everybody Loves a Good Apocalypse," *Reason*, October 24, 2015
10. German Lopez, "How Americans Think the World Will End," *Vox*, March 12, 2015.
11. Daniel Wojcik, *The End of the World as We Know It: Faith, Fatalism and Apocalypse in America*, New York University Press, 1999.
12. Richard Landes, *Heaven on Earth: The Varieties of the Millennial Experience*, Oxford University Press, 2011.
13. Michael Barkun, "Millennium Culture: The Year 2000 as a Religious Event," in *Millennial Visions: Essays on Twentieth Century Millernarianism*, ed. Martha F. Lee, Praeger, 2000.
14. Catherine Wessinger, *How the Millennium Comes Violently: From Jonestown to Heaven's Gate*, Seven Bridges Press, 1999.
15. German Lopez, "How Americans Think the World Will End, In Charts," *Vox*, March 12, 2015.
16. Wojcik, *The End of the World as We Know It*.
17. Kathleen Stewart and Susan Harding, "Bad Endings: American Apocalypsis," *Annual Review of Anthropology*, 28, 1999.
18. Lee Quinby, *Anti-Apocalypse: Exercises in Genealogical Criticism*, Minneapolis: University of Minnesota Press, 1994.
19. Quinby, *Anti-Apocalypse*.
20. Quinby, *Anti-Apocalypse*.
21. Stewart and Harding, "Bad Endings."
22. Solnit, *Hope in the Dark*.
23. Edward Ingebretsen, *At Stake: Monsters and the Rhetoric of Fear in Public Culture*, University of Chicago Press, 2001.
24. Edward Ingebretsen, *At Stake*.

3. "IT'S GOING TO BE A FEDERAL INCIDENT."

1. Ali S. Khan, "Preparedness 101: Zombie Apocalypse," Centers for Disease Control and Prevention's Public Health Matters Blog, May 16, 2011.
2. Chris Good, "Why Did the CDC Develop a Plan for the Zombie Apocalypse?" *The Atlantic*, May 20, 2011.
3. Khan, "Preparedness 101: Zombie Apocalypse."
4. Whitaker, "How Harold Camping Marketed the Rapture."
5. Caitlin Dickson, "Harold Camping Spent $100 million on Rapture Ads," *The Atlantic Wire*, May 24, 2011.
6. "CDC 'Zombie Apocalypse' Disaster Campaign Crashes Website," Reuters, May 19, 2011.
7. "Social Media: Preparedness 101: Zombie Apocalypse," Centers for Disease Control and Prevention, no date.
8. "Zombie Apocalypse: 'The Zombies Are Coming,' Homeland Security Warns," *The Huffington Post*, September 6, 2012.
9. Julie Watson, "'Zombie Apocalypse' Training Drill Organized by Halo Corp. For Military Police Set for October 31 in San Diego," *The Huffington Post*, October 27, 2012.
10. Caroline May, "Homeland Security grants went to 'zombie apocalypse' training," *The Daily Caller*, December 5, 2012.
11. Neil MacFarquhar, "As Domestic Terrorists Outpace Jihadists, New U.S. Law Is Debated," *The New York Times*, February 25, 2020.
12. Zolan Kanno-Youngs, "Homeland Security Dept. Affirms Threat of White Supremacy After Years of Prodding," *The New York Times*, October 1, 2019.

4. "NO JOKE, THE ZOMBIE APOCALYPSE IS COMING!"

1. Mira Grant, *Blackout*, Orbit Books, 2012.
2. "Ronald Poppo, victim of face chewing attacker, tells cops Rudy Eugene 'ripped me to ribbons,'" *CBS News*, August 9, 2012 and

"Rudy Eugene, Fla. 'face-chewer,' had no flesh in stomach, autopsy says," *CBS News*, June 12, 2012.
3. Tracey Parece, "Cannibal who ate man's face alleged victim of Voodoo curse not bath salts drug," *The Examiner*, June 1, 2012.
4. Seni Tienabeso, "Mother of Miami 'Cannibal' Says Son Was Drugged Before Alleged Attack," *ABC World News*, May 31, 2012.
5. "Rudy Eugene's mother: Son was no 'zombie,' should have been tased not shot," *CBS News*, May 31, 2012.
6. Tracey Parece, "Was Danny Bonaduce the latest victim of a zombie attack?", *The Examiner*, October 1, 2012.
7. S.L. Schmitz, "Was George A. Romero Right All Along?", *The Examiner*, June 3, 2012.
8. Zombie Instances, Google Map, May 2012.
9. Tony Dokoupil, "Could the Internet Bring on a Zombie Apocalypse?", *The Daily Beast*, June 11, 2012.
10. S.L. Schmitz, "Zombie experts weigh in on the zombie apocalypse," *The Examiner*, June 5, 2012.
11. Zomboid, June 27, 2012 (12:37 p.m.), comment on Chris Scullin, "Zombie Apocalypse," *UWeekly*, June 27, 2012.
12. Andy Campbell, "Zombie Apocalypse: The CDC Denies Existence of Zombies Despite Cannibal Incidents," *The Huffington Post*, June 1, 2012.

5. "ARE YOU ABLE TO SHOOT YOUR KID IN THE FACE?"

1. Spencer Ackerman, "Army's Disaster Prep Now Includes Tips From the Zombie Apocalypse," *Wired*, April 12, 2013.
2. Sarah Fisch, "Unprepared for the Undead?", *San Antonio Magazine*, January 2012.
3. Morgan Barnhart, *Could the Zombie Apocalypse Become Reality? An In-Depth Look at Four Real-Life Possibilities*, Zombie Research Team, 2012), Kindle edition.
4. Richard Laycock, "Doomsday Prepper Statistics," *Finder*, no date.

5. Matt Bemer, "How Much a Zombie Apocalypse Survival Kit Costs," *Money*, February 21, 2016.
6. Tim Murphy, "Preppers Are Getting Ready for the Barackalypse," *Mother Jones*, December 20, 2012.
7. Roz Zurko, "Zombie Apocalypse: very real to those stockpiling food and guns," *The Examiner*, June 3, 2012.
8. Neil Genzlinger, "Girding for Zombies," *New York Times*, December 17, 2012.
9. Patrick Kevin Day, "Discovery's 'Zombie Apocalypse' plays what-if with end times," *Los Angeles Times*, Dec. 28, 2012.

6. "WE HATE ALL ZOMBIES."

1. Regina Wang, "Long Island Man Shoots Girlfriend over The Walking Dead, Post-Apocalyptic Style," *Time*, December 6, 2012.
2. Bridget Murphy, "Nassau man gets prison for 'zombie' shooting," *Newsday*, February 6, 2014.
3. "Apocalypse Kit," Gerber Gear, no date.
4. Henry Miller Outdoors, "Zombie the new it word in hunting gear," *Statesman Journal*, December 6, 2012
5. "Zombies a Factor in Gun Sales Increase, Gun Rights Advocates Say," *The Huffington Post*, December 3, 2012.
6. Alan Farnham, "Gun Sales Booming: Doomsday, Obama, or Zombies?", *ABC News*, April 5, 2012,.
7. Marc Herman, "Gun Owners Are Obsessed with Zombies," *Salon*, February 21, 2013.
8. Benny Johnson, "National Rifle Association Bans Bleeding "Obama" Target, Others Remain," BuzzFeed, May 5, 2013.
9. Eli Epstein, "Did the NRA ban zombie targets that resemble Obama?", *MSN News*, May 7, 2013.
10. Epstein, "Did the NRA ban zombie targets that resemble Obama?"
11. "Zombie Ex-Girlfriend Shooting Target Awakens Controversy," *The Huffington Post*, April 3, 2013.

12. Terri Hamrick, Domestic Violence Awareness Month: What a Week Without Domestic Abuse Would Look Like," *USA Today*, October 26, 2019.
13. The Giffords Law Center, "Domestic Violence and Firearms."
14. German Lopez and Kavya Sukumar, "Mass Shootings Since Sandy Hook," *Vox*, updated on May 6, 2020
15. "2019 Police Shootings Database," *The Washington Post*, updated May 1, 2020.
16. Laura Santhanam, "After Ferguson, black men still face the highest risk of being killed by police," *PBS Newshour*, August 9, 2019.
17. Patrik Jonnson, "With gun violence down, is America arming against an imagined threat?' *Christian Science Monitor*, May 8, 2013.
18. Phillip Bump, "Most Americans incorrectly think gun-murder rates have gotten worse, not better," *The Washington Post*, February 14, 2019.
19. Bump, "Most Americans incorrectly think gun-murder rates…" and Bill Chappell, "Rate Of U.S. Gun Violence Has Fallen Since 1993, Study Says," NPR, May 7, 2013.

AFTERWORD: "YOU'VE GOT SOME RED ON YOU."

1. Kelly J. Baker, "Zombies, Millennialism, and Consumption," *Religion in American History*, January 21, 2011.
2. Brian Chappell, "The Zombie Apocalypse," Facebook, Accessed May 25, 2013.
3. Ingebretsen, *At Stake*.

ACKNOWLEDGMENTS

It's a unique privilege for a writer to be able to have a second go at a book and see how you can make it better the next time around. Or at least, you aim to make it better when you return to the material. So, it's no surprise that I jumped at the opportunity to not only update but also expand this book, first published in 2013. I first started revisions in 2018 and put them down. And picked them up in 2019 and put them down. And finally finished them in 2020. There was an urgency to finishing them amid a pandemic because I thought zombies have something to tell us about what's happening right now.

It might seem strange to talk of monsters in a world that seems to constantly be on fire, but it's not. There are things to learn from these monstrous messengers about our world and about ourselves. Remember, always remember, monsters warn. We should hear what they have say. It only took me ten years to really stop and listen to the zombies, so I hope reading this book means that y'all catch on faster than I did.

When you work on a project for ten years, a lot of people help you out along the way. Or at least, that was the case for me. I can't remember everyone who helped me out. Thank you to all of you, who helped even if you didn't know you were.

There are some folks who deserve special recognition. *The Zombies Are Coming* first and foremost exists because of the students in my 2010 course, The Apocalypse in American Culture, at the University of Tennessee. These students were the ones who pulled my attention toward zombies and the comments they made and the questions they asked stuck with me. I started researching zombies because of them, and I'm (mostly) glad I did.

This book, however, wouldn't have come into being without the urging of Patton Dodd, the former executive editor of Bondfire Books, which sadly no longer exists. Patton asked me if I had a project on religion and American culture, so I pitched him a book on zombies. He accepted it, so I wrote it. Thanks, Patton, for giving me the excuse to take a hard look at the zombie apocalypse and why it matters.

I was lucky to have an amazing group of people, who helped me think through the arguments in this book and cheered me on as I finished it—Sean McCloud, Anthony

Santoro, Katja Rakow, Katie Lofton, Jason Bivins, Moxy Moczygemba, Shreena Gandhi, Matt Cressler, and Richard Newton. Megan Goodwin, Katie Guest Pryal, and Miguel Clark Mallet helped convince me to finish this damn book by being tireless supporters. They wouldn't let me quit even when I wanted to. You were able to read this book because of them. Thanks, y'all.

Lauren Faulkenberry is an editor extraordinaire, and she convinced me to take a no holds bar approach to the book. She was so right, and any faults in this book are completely my own.

My family has allowed me to keep up this scholarly fascination with zombies for a decade without batting an eye. That's how I know they love me. Thank you to my siblings, Stephanie, Ashley, and Cary. And thanks especially to my parents, Dottie and Steve, for encouraging me to do my best even if my best is writing about the undead.

My kids, Kara and Ethan, have long accepted that their mom writes about creepy things like zombies, and they really seem to enjoy telling people that I wrote a book about zombies just to see how folks react. While I might have started thinking about zombies and apocalypses because of my students, I kept researching and writing about the end of the world because of my kids. I want a better world to be possible not only for them but also for the rest of us. We deserve so much more than the bleak end of the world that the people in this book look forward to.

(Also, Kara wants me to thank our cats, Trick and Treat, so thank you, kitty boys, for walking across my laptop and causing all kinds of mayhem and distraction.)

And finally, thank you to Chris Baker, my partner and best friend. He's my first reader and best supporter. I couldn't have written this book or any of my others without him. I would fight zombies for you, Chris. I love you that much.

ABOUT THE AUTHOR

Award-winning author Kelly J. Baker is a freelance writer with a religious studies PhD who covers religion, racism, higher education, gender, labor, motherhood, and popular culture. She's written for *The New York Times*, *The Atlantic*, *The Rumpus*, *Chronicle Vitae*, *Religion & Politics*, *Killing the Buddha*, and *The Washington Post* among others.

Her first book, *Gospel According to the Klan: The KKK's Appeal to Protestant America, 1915-1930* (University Press of Kansas, 2011), won the American Library Association Choice Award in 2012. Her second book, *Grace Period: A Memoir in Pieces* (Blue Crow Books, 2017), details her life as a mother on the fringes of academia. Her third book, *Sexism Ed: Essays on Gender and Labor in Academia* (2017), won the Foreword INDIES Gold award for Women's Studies. Her latest book, *The Zombies Are Coming: The Realities of the Zombie Apocalypse in American Culture* (Revised and Expanded Edition, Blue Crow

Books, 2020), is the culmination of many years' research on apocalypses and zombies.

She's the editor of *Women in Higher Education*, a feminist newsletter, in its 26th year, with the continued goal "to enlighten, encourage, empower and enrage women on campus," and the *The National Teaching and Learning Forum*.

Kelly lives in Florida, the wildest state in the U.S., with her partner and two kids. When she's not writing, wrangling for kids or looking out for alligators, she's working her way toward a collection of essays about endings and other apocalypses.

- facebook.com/kellyjeanettebaker
- twitter.com/kelly_j_baker
- instagram.com/kelly_j_baker
- goodreads.com/kelly_j_baker
- bookbub.com/authors/kelly-j-baker
- amazon.com/author/kellyjbaker

CPSIA information can be obtained
at www.ICGtesting.com
Printed in the USA
LVHW091456300720
661951LV00002B/56